Responses to *Tales of a Century-Old Courthouse: New Madrid County, Missouri:*

"Life and death, tragedy and triumph—it all happens at the county court house. This vivid look back at the importance of the iconic New Madrid courthouse is a journey into the past we cannot forget."

Judge John R. O'Malley, retired,
Kansas City, Missouri

"I found the book a lively local history of a town seen through the lens of the county courthouse, where people came together, not only to resolve disputes but also to build a sense of community, seek refuge from natural calamities, and record their efforts for the benefit of posterity."

David Thomas Konig
Professor of History and Professor of Law
Washington University
St. Louis, Missouri

"The year 2015 found the New Madrid County Courthouse celebrating its centennial year, marking the construction that began in 1915. This is more than nostalgic to me since I began the practice of law in this courthouse half that many years ago in 1965. While the officeholders have come and gone, it has been a delight and pleasure to watch this stately building age in a respectable and dignified manner. I am immensely proud of the everyday experience of plying my trade in this grand old courthouse."

Lawrence H. Rost
Attorney At Law
New Madrid, Missouri

"Mary Sue Anton is an extraordinary historical researcher. Her first book, *New Madrid: A Mississippi River Town in History and Legend*, is a collection of both scholarly and grassroots research that illuminates the town's past like no other. This book follows in that tradition, combining official records with quotations from those citizens—from judges to 'suffragettes' and more—who are part of New Madrid's fascinating story."

Susan Swartwout, PhD
Professor of English, Southeast Missouri State University
Cape Girardeau, Missouri

Tales of a Century-Old Courthouse:
New Madrid County, Missouri

© 2016 Mary Sue Anton

All rights reserved. No part of this book may be reproduced or transmitted in any form or by any means, electronic or mechanical or by any information or storage and retrieval system without permission in writing from the author or publisher.

Published by
AKA-Publishing
Columbia, Missouri 65203

ISBN: 978-1-942168-42-3 Trade Paper

ISBN: 978-1-942168-45-4 eBook

Tales of a Century-Old Courthouse:
New Madrid County, Missouri

Mary Sue Anton

*At his best, man is the noblest of all animals;
separated from law and justice he is the worst.*

~ Aristotle

Dedication

To my maternal grandfather, Judge Lee C. Phillips who served as county clerk for New Madrid County from 1895 to 1906 and as probate judge from 1931 to 1939. Granddad Phillips was a kind and considerate gentleman and always tipped his hat to the ladies. He once had a Reo automobile, "one of the few cars in town," and, as he headed to the courthouse he would stop and ask any pedestrian if a ride downtown were needed.

Between serving as county clerk and probate judge, Phillips was a farmer, merchant, Laforge postmaster, and real estate dealer. At the turn of the 20th century, several New Madridians acquired "gold fever." In 1902, he traveled to Idaho and "spaded 3 ½ hours and found $4.50 of the virgin metal."[1] He later bought an interest in a gold mine in Montana. A slice of this property remains in the family.[2] Then again, one granddaughter said, "He lost his shirt."[3] Another quoted him as saying, "It is easy to become a millionaire but hard to hold on to it."[4]

Phillips once negotiated the sale of 82,000 acres of "one of the finest tracts of timber in Louisiana" to the Singer Sewing Company. While inspecting the virgin forest, he sustained a hip injury from which he never recovered. J.A. Parker, a friend, said that despite the "gigantic proposition," Phillips realized little profit after surveying and labor expenses.[5]

In 1893, the county court appointed Phillips, F.R. Yount and Lee Hunter to serve as drainage commissioners.[6] In early July they went to the spot where the Little River Drainage District work would begin and drove a golden spike, thus mimicking railroad men of the day.[7] In 1908 Phillips served as first secretary for the District under Chairman Sen. R.B. Oliver.[8] In addition, he drew up sketches for an earthwork front levee at New Madrid and worked tirelessly to get it implemented in 1916 despite many arguments against it.

At his funeral in 1941, Phillips was eulogized as a person who gave of himself for others.[9] A self-taught surveyor, Phillips laid out the expansive Main Street in the little town of Portageville, "due to his vision of the future." [10] In the early 1900s, he donated land on Highway 62 East just outside Malden for a one-room schoolhouse. After school consolidation in the 1950s, the square, red-brick school served as a community building and later, a church. The building was demolished in the 1990s.

In the 1920s, Phillips visited pecan groves all over the south looking for the perfect pecan and, stopping at Sherard, Mississippi, learned about the commercial value of the pecan and also how to top-graft native stocks. He subsequently grafted 100 acres on overflow land alongside St. John Bayou, known then as "the bottoms." He had found his niche. My family inherited the grove plus trees on the Phillips home place. In the 1950s and 1960s, most fall weekends, people from the area descended in droves on my parents' home on East Dawson Road and crossed the levee to gather paper-shell and native pecans on the shares. Some of these trees are still producing.

It gets better: today, one can order a Shy's Pecan Orchard sundae at Pink's Ice Cream Parlor on Main Street. Look what entrepreneur Probate Judge Lee C. Phillips has wrought.

Granddad Phillips is just one example of all the dedicated men and women who have worked tirelessly making New Madrid the county it is today.

Contents

    Dedication   i
    Foreword   v
    Preface   vii

Chapter 1
    Courthouse Architecture   1

Chapter 2
    Centennial Celebration   3

Chapter 3
    Beginnings   7

Chapter 4
    The Original County Seal   10

Chapter 5
    Pioneer Court Proceedings   12

Chapter 6
    A Proper Seat of Justice   15

Chapter 7
    The Restless River   17

Chapter 8
    Challenges of Fire and Floods   19

Chapter 9
    Courthouse Square Park   21

Chapter 10
    Construction Delays   24

Chapter 11
    A Well Deserved Dedication   27

Chapter 12
    Our Officials' Finest Hour   29

Chapter 13
    Disaster on the Mississippi   35

Photos
    Photos   39

Chapter 14
    The Workings of the County   65
Chapter 15
    Other Homes in the Courthouse   87
    Conclusion   92
    Acknowledgments   94
Appendices
    Endnotes   97
    Bibliography   111
    Interviews/Facebook   115

Foreword

With the aging of nineteenth and early twentieth century courthouses across Missouri, the histories and architecture of these buildings have become a frequent focus of historians. Some counties have worked to preserve their buildings, while others have preferred demolition and new buildings to serve the needs of their county citizens. This struggle between preservationists and pragmatists continues to challenge counties across Missouri that want to meet the needs of their citizens and physically recognize their heritage. During its 226-year history, New Madrid County has traveled along both paths. But today, the heritage of preserving its 1915 courthouse has come to the forefront.

County government is the oldest business in New Madrid County. Following the history through Mary Sue Anton's book of New Madrid County takes us on a journey from a remote frontier outpost in 1789 to a well-run, progressive, and leading rural Missouri county in 2015. The centuries-long journey from a primitive log cabin to a modern, multistoried stone and brick building is a history of government. But, as Anton notes, New Madrid County has faced many challenges while growing from a frontier outpost on the unstable banks of the Mississippi River.

When Mark Twain visited New Madrid* in 1882, he said, "The town . . . was looking very unwell, but otherwise unchanged from its former condition and aspect." He failed to note that in the twenty plus years between his visits, the river had pushed the town back nearly half a mile. This included the courthouse, which had relocated from its near-river perch twice during that period. The recent 1882 flood had inundated the town. Unwell indeed.

Today, citizens come and go at the courthouse as if it has been there forever. But as we learn from Mary Sue Anton, there was great struggle and sacrifice to build it, and we need to remember and recognize that effort.

The 2015 centennial anniversary of the New Madrid County Courthouse is as proper a time as any to explore the rich history of our government and its meeting places. The author highlights the events of that history down to present times.

Taken care of properly, the courthouse will continue to serve the citizens of our county for many years to come. Readers of this volume who visit the building will find much more to admire and remember.

H. Riley Bock
New Madrid, Missouri
December 2015

*Mark Twain. *Life on the Mississippi*. Harper & Brothers, New York (1917), 223.

Preface

Today, looking up at the impressive building at 450 Main Street in New Madrid, Missouri, one sees an elegant structure known to all as "The Courthouse." However, accommodations for conducting county business were not always as elaborate as those found in New Madrid today. In trying to apply the law with fairness to people living on the edge of civilization, New Madrid's first magistrates conferred and held elections in private homes, probably rough-hewn log cabins with puncheon floors. Settlers' crude homes took advantage of the shade of abundant trees. Typically, one room was used for cooking and the other for living and sleeping. Simple cabins had one door plus a window admitting light. A fireplace provided warmth and a means for cooking. During harsh winters, people gathered close around the fireplace. The cabins were drafty, so it is likely that the judges, especially those of French descent, dressed for warmth in a *capote*—a long cloak with a hood, usually made from a blanket. The hood could be worn down around the shoulders or up over the head.[11]

When the weather turned warm, a covered breezeway with its bare earth floor provided a welcome respite from the heat. Perhaps in those early days, court was held outside under leafy trees when the summer heat became almost unbearable. It is difficult for us to imagine this scene, as we take for granted that our court business and government functions are carried out in grand, modern buildings.

During the Spanish regime, commandants appointed by a Louisiana province governor took on numerous responsibilities. In addition to applying justice in a wilderness, they attended to the welfare of residents in other ways.

In the middle of the summer of 1789, Don Estevan Miró, governor of the Spanish American province of Louisiana, appointed Don Pedro Foucher as New Madrid commandant. A commandant was given political and military command of a settlement. He was to encourage population growth and agriculture, as well as "preserve by all possible means, good relations, peace and quietness among these new colonists, and administer justice to them with the mildness and gentleness peculiar to our government." [12] The commandants met in Fort Céleste on the river, or in their own homes. In 1796, Commandant Tomas Portell forwarded residents' oaths of allegiance to His Catholic Majesty, that they would live under his laws and "were ready to take up arms if necessary." [13]

Illinois Lieutenant Governor Zenon Trudeau wrote from St. Louis in 1794 that the mortality rate in New Madrid was high due to pneumonia. The problem was "the badly-founded preconception of some against bleeding, and the lack of a bloodletter for others." [14] Medical knowledge was primitive in those days.

After Creek Indians murdered a farmer in January 1802, Commandant Henri Peyroux prohibited trading of any kind with them. Five were captured and sent in a galley to New Orleans for sentencing by the governor-general.[15] The "principal culprit" received a death sentence and was executed a year later in New Madrid.[16]

As the current New Madrid courthouse building turned 100 years old in 2015, most of the county celebrated this milestone. However, I have discovered much more to the story. My hope is that history will never grow stale, and these stories will be preserved for the future. I hope to spark my readers' imagination and give them an incentive to go into the courthouse and see for themselves what treasures and revelations are squirreled away.

I pored over old court records, wills, and deed records, and tried to resurrect the human stories they represent. I wanted to introduce a few stories by writing a book, thus giving at least a segment of New Madrid County's records a second home.

I examined many records, trying to digest and understand things that seem strange, and yes, horrifying, to us today, such as our ancestors buying and selling slaves, and, as recently as the early 1950s, the signs on the doors to the rest rooms in the courthouse proclaiming, "White Ladies Only" or "White Men Only."

Yes, that was the way it was back then, in New Madrid and in many other places all across America, but of course that did not make it right. This book provides insights into some of the dreadful mistakes our ancestors made, in addition to their marvelous achievements, not always under the best of situations. Hopefully, this book will inspire future generations to greatness.

Mary Sue Anton

Chapter 1

Courthouse Architecture

At the corner of Virginia and Main Streets, in the middle of New Madrid, Missouri, looms a white sandstone and white glazed brick building erected in the Classical Greek Revival style. The main entrance of the 100-year-old building faces east, where two classic columns towering twenty-six feet, each with a diameter of nearly three feet, flank the portico. In keeping with the county's primary industry, agriculture, eight strings of three opened cotton bolls hang from the scrolling volutes at the top, or capital, of the column. In describing the courthouse, local historian and attorney H. Riley Bock writes,

> "Another allusion to the county's agricultural heritage is a traditional design draped on the doorway and windows in the portico which contains a familiar mixture of acorns, leaves and fruits. The cotton bolls are unique."[17]

Cotton became king in southeast Missouri after drainage of the swamplands in the 1920s. Although corn seemed to have been the principal crop in the early part of the century, the teen years may have been the transition period to cotton. Ryan Eddy, executive director of the New Madrid County Farm Service Agency says,

"Approximately twenty percent of cropland in New Madrid County is planted to cotton. This is an approximate amount, and varies from year to year. This amount would apply only to New Madrid County. Depending on which counties in 'southeast' Missouri are considered in this definition, the percentage of cotton grown can vary tremendously." [18]

The courthouse features marble stairways with cast-iron railings. For almost a century, footsteps and voices have echoed across the hexangular-tiled floors and drifted up a large rotunda under an elegant, stained-glass dome. Residents consider the courthouse a trophy that gives them a sense of identity.

It is probably no coincidence that county officials usually place a courthouse in the middle of town or on the town square. A courthouse is a symbol of government power, and it illustrates the might of the justice system. Often the largest building in town—as is the three-story New Madrid courthouse—the imposing structure stands for law and order.

A courthouse also presents a human side. It serves as a gathering place where citizens meet friends and neighbors while conducting crucial transactions, such as attending to a civil or criminal case, applying for marriage licenses, obtaining death certificates, or paying taxes. Here gossip and news of importance is passed on. In some towns, residents—usually retired—take advantage of benches to sit, visit, whittle, and convey tall tales. And in New Madrid, a wide expanse of shady lawn enhanced by well-tended gardens and landscaping gives tourists an opportunity to snap pictures of a century-old courthouse with their smart phones or digital cameras.

In the meantime, the "prim and proper" courthouse has been the brunt of many a joke. Does anyone remember how, in the early 1950s, a Model T always seemed to appear on the east side steps every year on the day after Halloween? It is said that one year a "two-holer" showed up. You know who you are—or who it was.

Chapter 2

Centennial Celebration

In the spring of 2014, New Madrid County Presiding Commissioner Mark Baker and Associate Commissioners Don Day and Tom Bradley decided to celebrate the courthouse centennial throughout the year 2015. They appointed Riley Bock to oversee a Courthouse Centennial Committee to plan and carry out the festivities. Ten people came forward to serve: Lynn H. Bock, Amy Brown, Sarah Ezell, Aaron Griffin, Marsha Holiman, Timmie Lynn Hunter, Ed Riley, Larry Rost, Paula Scobey, and Ronnie Simmons.

Riley explained that construction of this courthouse began in 1915, but World War I delayed its completion until 1919. He added, "The building has several unique architectural features, and has hosted several important state and national events, including senatorial campaign speeches in 1934 and 1940 by future president Harry S. Truman." [19]

President Truman often spent the night with New Madrid County Prosecuting Attorney J.V. Conran. One morning in the late 1940s, my brother Robert, and sister Alice, recall seeing a car back out of Conran's driveway on Main Street. Someone in the back seat waved, and my father pulled over to the curb and asked them if they knew who that guy was. Of course they didn't, so my father leaned over the seat and told them,[20] "That is the President of the United States!"

A Truman marker was dedicated in front of the courthouse during the centennial. The following words were lifted from the marker: "The 1940 campaign speech declared that national defense would be his priority. Truman's second senate nomination in 1940 was supported by J.V. Conran, a strong ally in that very close Senate primary race." Truman said,

> "I am deeply affected that the good people of a part of Missouri most remote from my home town did me such a singular honor."

In preparation for the centennial celebration, the courthouse was cleaned, tuck-pointed, and painted. In addition, the stained-glass dome was repaired and relit.[21]

In 2015, the Committee published and distributed a commemorative calendar including photos and facts about the construction of the 1915 courthouse and a few personalities from that era.

The Centennial Committee also struck a Centennial medallion that depicts the county seal as described in Chapter 4. It is available for purchase in silver at the Higgerson Landing Gift Shop on Main Street. Both the New Madrid Historical Museum and this gift shop offer a handsome 1915 – 2015 Centennial Christmas ornament.

On display at the courthouse and along Main Street were banners complete with the original gold and silver courthouse seals. The courthouse's first and second floor exhibits focus on the history of the building itself.

A party at the courthouse, hosted by the Committee, kicked off the Centennial festivities in January 2015. State, county and city elected officials, attorneys, judges, and county workers were among the invitees. In addition, community leaders and descendants of some of the founding fathers gathered to celebrate.

The Committee had installed life-size reproductions of portraits of three of the county's founders, Robert D. Dawson, Robert

Goah Watson and John Hardeman Walker on the second floor.

Dawson came to New Madrid in 1800 and, in 1815 and 1816, represented New Madrid in the General Assembly of the Territory. He served as a member of the convention of 1820 held in St. Louis, which drafted the first constitution of the state of Missouri.[22]

Watson, "for half a century one of the leading merchants in New Madrid," arrived there in 1804.[23] He served as county court judge from 1821-22 and again from 1824-34.[24]

Walker came to Little Prairie in 1810,[25] just before the big earthquakes. He served as New Madrid's sheriff from 1821 to 1822 and county representative from 1846 to 1848.[26] Douglas writes that "several 'leading' citizens . . . among whom were Col. John H. [Hardeman] Walker and Representative Stephen Ross, by exerting their influence, succeeded in having the line from the Mississippi to the St. Francois [rivers] lowered to the parallel of 36°." [27] Thus, Missouri acquired the Bootheel, an area encompassing 627,000 acres.

In February 1821, the county court appointed Colonel Walker as guardian for two children of John Ordway, a key Lewis and Clark expedition member who had died.[28] After receiving his acreage from the expedition, Ordway exchanged and purchased more land in the fertile Tywappity Bottoms. He bought several lots in New Madrid [29] but it is not known if he ever lived in New Madrid.

In April 2015, Centennial Committee members, county commissioners and the Missouri Conservation Department staff met on the courthouse lawn and planted three new trees. County Assessor Ronnie Simmons had solicited help from the Conservation Department. Forrester Ross Glenn described the trees being planted: two flowering dogwoods, the Missouri state tree, one of which was planted at the front corner of the east lawn and the other in the back lawn. The third tree is a bur oak, another tree native to New Madrid and proven to be drought resistant and tough. The bur oak was planted on the front lawn next to Virginia Street where a large tree once stood.

Centennial Committee Chairman Bock said,

> "At one time New Madrid County was completely forested. Harvesting trees during the first part of the twentieth century was a big deal. The previous generation drained the swamp, harvested the trees and turned it all into farmland. So, in a way, planting trees on the courthouse lawn is quite symbolic because it links us to our forest past." [30]

On December 31, 2015, in frigid temperatures and high winds the tenacious Centennial Committee unveiled a marker for President Truman and two historical panels on the courthouse lawn. To help defray centennial expenses, a gold medallion was raffled off. New Madrid's Greg Crisler was the winner.

The Centennial Committee invited citizens, and especially school children, to take this opportunity to learn more about their heritage.[31]

Chapter 3

Beginnings

Historian Louis Houck writes that fur traders and first permanent settlers Joseph and Francois LeSieur "must be considered the founders of the New Madrid settlement." Gabriel Cerré, the principal merchant of St. Louis, had sent the LeSieurs to "L'Anse à la Graisse" in 1783.[32] The trading post was called "L'Anse à la Graisse"—or cove of fat or grease—because of the abundance of game, especially bears and buffaloes.[33]

When Revolutionary War patriot George Morgan founded New Madrid in 1789, he named it "Nuevo Madrid" to curry favor with Spanish Royalty. Today, the town and county of the same name are officially pronounced "New MAD-rid." After George Morgan left New Madrid to return to his native Pennsylvania, the Spaniards chose a commandant to take civil and military command. Commandant Pierre Foucher, a Frenchman who could not speak English, administered local government and answered directly to New Orleans. Houck writes,

> "The people were not allowed to participate in public affairs. Politics and politicians were unknown. The Commandant was supposed to look after matters concerning the welfare of the community." [34]

The Spanish commandant in St. Louis, Carlos DeHault DeLassus, followed Foucher as New Madrid's commandant, and was succeeded by Don Henri Peyroux and Don Juan LaVallee.

Early New Madrid archives, written in either French or English, were deposited with the Missouri Historical Society (MHS) in St. Louis in 1908 by order of the county court. Then, in 1940, the Society published "Index to the New Madrid Archives (1791-1804." Some of these records have yet to be translated into the English language. One example of court proceedings was an Agreement dated April 6, 1802 when French Commandant Henry Peyroux appointed school teacher Louis Baby to hold Francois Riche Dupin's place as sacristan for St. Isidore Catholic Church until Dupin returned from a voyage to France.[35]

The Louisiana Purchase treaty was signed in April 1803, but it wasn't until the following spring that New Madrid residents realized they had become citizens of the United States. At this point, most orders for carrying out business in New Madrid originated in St. Louis.

New Madrid was one of the original five Spanish districts in "Louisiana." [36] Other districts were St. Louis, St. Charles, Ste. Genevieve, and Cape Girardeau. In June 1812, Upper Louisiana was called the Missouri Territory.

The New Madrid District became a county on October 1, 1812. In 1815, the Territorial Legislature began establishing boundary lines for other counties within the vast New Madrid County, which extended south through Arkansas.[37] The twenty-nine counties carved out of the New Madrid District were: Scott, Mississippi, New Madrid, Pemiscot, Dunklin, Stoddard, Butler, Carter, Oregon, Ripley, Howell, Christian, Douglas, Clark, Taney, Stone, and Barry. It also included parts of the counties of Bollinger, Wayne, Reynolds, Shannon, Texas, Wright,

Webster, Greene, Lawrence, Jasper, Newton, and McDonald." [38]

In 1939, historian Floyd Calvin Shoemaker described New Madrid as "in all probability, the first American city west of the Mississippi River." [39] Shoemaker was the third secretary of the State Historical Society of Missouri (SHSM), and he served for forty-five years. The term for this position eventually evolved to director, which is used today.

Chapter 4

The Original County Seal

The following words about the county seal tell about courthouse burnings, seals lost, records lost, and the Centennial Committee's resurrection of the 1821 seal. These words appear on one of two historic panels in front of the courthouse:

*New Madrid County 1821 Seal
As described by the Courthouse Centennial Committee
January 2015* [40]

Adopted by the County Court after statehood was granted, the seal features the American eagle as it was depicted at the time, with twenty-four stars. Missouri became the 24th state of the Union on August 10, 1821.

The seal was used for official county business until it was destroyed in the courthouse fire on Sunday, September 24, 1905. After the fire, county offices quickly relocated into several buildings on New Madrid's Main Street. For reasons unknown—perhaps the rush to resume county business—the 1905 replacement seal omitted the eagle, stars, and the date 1821.

A description of the seal contained in the May 1821 County Court minute book—before statehood—did not include the date 1821, and had a ring of only twenty stars around the eagle.[41] The significance, if any, of the twenty stars is not clear, which may

Chapter 4: The Original County Seal

explain their elimination. It is not known how long that seal was used before it was altered to include the twenty-four stars and the date 1821. The twenty-four stars are the same as in the Great Seal of the State of Missouri, which was approved in January 1822.

It was not until 2014 that a good impression of the 1821 seal was discovered on several 1890s county court documents that had fallen behind the drawer of an old file cabinet in the attic of the courthouse. These documents provided sufficient evidence to reconstruct the seal. The County Commission readopted the 1821 seal as its official seal in November 2014.

This cast aluminum seal measures twenty inches in diameter. The American eagle is depicted in the same colors used on the Great Seal of the State of Missouri.

Chapter 5

Pioneer Court Proceedings

"By 1804," writes Shoemaker, "the Americans were a significant element of the population. They were generally law-abiding because they both dreaded and respected the enforcement of Spanish criminal law, because they were independent and self-reliant, and perhaps because their location on isolated farms resulted in fewer conflicts and less friction . . . . They were satisfied with Spanish rule . . . and they were not particularly happy about the change to American control in 1804." [42]

On the other hand, Houck writes that during Spanish rule, many residents were of French descent. They "lived in the midst of plenty where it was easy to make a livelihood," and began to build houses that were "substantially and warmly built of vertically placed planks or hewn logs, chinked with clay or stone." [43]

New Madrid formally organized its courts in March 1805. Serving in New Madrid's Court of Common Pleas and Quarter-Sessions of the Peace[44] were two of my ancestors. Richard Jones Waters, "a physician by trade" from Maryland, joined New Madrid founder George Morgan in the late 1700s in Louisville,[45] and Jean Baptiste Olive was "one of a few emigrants who came to New Madrid directly from France." [46] After the Louisiana Purchase, Waters "was a leading and active member of the first convention assembled west of the Mississippi River, and his name

Chapter 5: Pioneer Court Proceedings

appears on the remonstrance addressed by that convention to the Congress of the United States." [47]

Robert Sidney Douglass writes that court records from the 1805 era have been destroyed, and "there is practically no information available concerning the work of this court." [48]

Today, the Missouri State Archives has made digitized collections of many court files available online.[49] In addition, private genealogy researchers have published some of the New Madrid court records which can be found in public libraries.

Shortly after the continuous big earthquakes of 1811-12, the idea of holding court in New Madrid was abandoned. In February 1812, Judge Michael Amoreaux (1805-12) removed official records and declared the New Madrid office "closed." [50]

In 1814, the reorganized Court of Common Pleas was composed of Thomas Neale, John LaVallee, William Winchester, and William Gray. For that spring session, the judges met at Samuel Phillips' house in Big Prairie, and convened next at the home of Jesse Bartlett.[51] Other common pleas judges not mentioned above were Dr. Henry Masters, Elisha Winsor, Dr. Samuel Dorsey, Joseph Hunter, and P.A. LaForge.[52]

Judge Richard S. Thomas organized the circuit court at William Montgomery's home in Big Prairie in December 1815. The first important case was the trial of William Gordon, who was charged with murder. Col. John Hardeman Walker was the sheriff, and Greer W. Davis was the circuit attorney. Davis likely rode in on a horse. Upon conviction, Gordon was hanged just below the town of Winchester,[53] near today's Sikeston.

In the fall of 1815, Stephen Ross and Moses Hurley donated an inland, fifty-acre plot one-fourth mile south of today's Sikeston for New Madrid's seat of justice. County surveyor Joseph Story laid off lots on the property, and money realized from the sale of lots was used to erect a jail, completed in 1817.[54]

The circuit court met at the courthouse in Rossville in October 1817, with Hon. Richard S. Thomas presiding as judge.[55] When the court met in April 1819, it was at the courthouse in the town of Winchester.[56]

Until the county seat returned to New Madrid, court divided its time between Winchester and Rossville.[57] Winchester,[58] located near today's Scott County line, eventually became known as Bayouville.

In August 1821, the New Madrid sheriff took possession of the courthouse in Winchester. His job was to supervise repairs, using private subscriptions or donations. At the same session, compensation for justices was fixed at $2 per day.[59]

Chapter 6

A Proper Seat of Justice

In October 1822, after Scott County was carved out of New Madrid County, the city of New Madrid once again became the county seat of justice. Commissioners Mark H. Stallcup, John Shanks, and Thomas Bartlett purchased property and inserted a notice in a Jackson newspaper justifying their reasons for keeping the county seat in New Madrid. The public notice emphasized that remarks "highly injurious to this country . . . totally false and unfounded" had been reported due to the earthquakes. A glowing description of the town's attributes followed, alongside advertisements for town lots:

> "The town of New Madrid is the only proper situation . . . The site is not far from the river, and is high, dry, and healthy . . . As healthy as any town situated on navigable fresh water . . . Diseases are few and seldom dangerous." [60]

After selling the old Rossville jail, commissioners Stallcup, Shanks, and Bartlett, along with Francois LeSieur and John Ruddell, built a log jail in New Madrid, with a small courthouse, "the first frame building in town." [61] The county had purchased and plotted a tract of land north of town. One block was set aside as a public square with Market Street on its west, where the courthouse faced. Other streets are listed, but the Mississippi River has long since obliterated any evidence of the old town.[62]

Chapter 7

The Restless River

A new jail was constructed in 1845, and the courthouse was replaced in 1854 [63] when contractors Frank Barclay and Christian Schultz erected a one-story frame structure. It was built at a cost of $2,750, under the supervision of County Treasurer T.J.O. Morrison.[64] Two offices on the north end and two on the south flanked the courtroom of the red-cypress building[65] located just north of Limit Street.[66]

In 1871, A.R. Waud of *Harper's Weekly* sketched the 1854 courthouse in a riverfront scene embellished with a docked flatboat.[67] The sketched location of the courthouse is not the original site. It was moved north on Jefferson Street (future Main) by the time this sketch was made. The building appears to have been moved to this location prior to 1862.[68]

Riley Bock conducted extensive research from deed records on the location of this "first" courthouse. So, today, we have a list of citizens whose property lay surrounding the "County Addition for Courthouse." [69] The river eventually consumed most of this property. The description can be found in the *Photos* section.

Specifications for a new jail in 1860, signed by Commissioner R.H. Hatcher, suggest that a number of inmates "engineered" escapes from the previous structure. The building was to be two stories high, with an upper story of oak plank four inches thick, securely spiked together, with two cells constructed of boiler iron three-sixteenths of an inch thick.[70]

During the Civil War, in February 1862, Confederates fortified New Madrid. The courthouse closed once again, and county officials removed many records for safekeeping. The following month, during the siege of New Madrid by Union soldiers, Confederates constructed an artillery platform on the top of the courthouse.[71]

In November 1874, with river banks closing in on the courthouse, the county court appointed Superintendent of Public Buildings David Emerson to acquire an acre of ground with a "front of fifty yards" either within the city of New Madrid, or just north, for a new courthouse site.[72]

In the spring of 1875, after purchasing a lot in Napoleon "Nap" B. Byrne's new addition, the court spent $400 to move the courthouse and jail to the southwest corner of Riley and Powell. The river was on the rampage again. The judges allotted $250 for repairs.[73]

Chapter 8

Challenges of Fire and Floods

Alas, while the Civil War battle spared the courthouse, a 1905 conflagration spelled its end. In the wee hours of a September Sunday morning, shouts from jail inmates awakened the sheriff's son, William Griffith, who gave the alarm. Griffith and the jailer, W.O. Shankle, fired their revolvers "rapidly" to awaken the neighborhood. As a large crowd stood by helplessly, flames soon reduced the wooden structure to ashes. County officials were able to salvage all records stored in fireproof vaults. The collector lost only some "old useless tax books," while the sheriff lost his fee book and subpoenas for the current court term, surely a pleasant surprise for several reprobates.

The jail, thirty to forty feet away, was "scorched but not badly injured," but officers removed and guarded the inmates until the danger passed. Only the heavy foliage of mulberry trees separating the courthouse and jail prevented the fire from devouring the second structure.[74]

Fourteen months before, an uncurbed fire destroyed ten business houses on Main Street.[75] No doubt, public servants now breathed sighs of relief, knowing that official records were secure in the new vaults.

Officials lost no time in relocating. J.W. Jackson, circuit clerk and recorder of deeds, found temporary quarters in the new Hunter

Bank Building, while County Clerk Lee C. Phillips moved into the New Madrid Banking Company's building. The "old" Peoples Bank building housed Probate Judge J.H. Bishop, Collector Henry E. Broughton, and Sheriff Thomas F. Henry.[76]

County officials had learned a lesson. In the spring of 1907, using 15,000 bricks, workmen built a fireproof vault in the "temporary courthouse," the Banking Company's brick building on Main Street.[77] In the meantime, Circuit Judge Henry C. Riley conducted court in the three-year-old [78] city hall.[79]

New Madrid's was one of many frame courthouses that went up in flames during the 19th and early 20th centuries. In 1864, Stoddard County lost its courthouse in Bloomfield to fire during the Civil War when some "stragglers" from Sterling Price's raid burned it down.[80] Even Cape Girardeau County's brick and stone courthouse fell victim to a fire in 1870.[81] Dunklin County's frame courthouse burned in 1872,[82] Pemiscot County's in December 1882,[83] and Butler County's in December 1886.[84] Frequent wintertime fires suggest that overheated stoves contributed to the infernos.

After the Pemiscot County courthouse burned to the ground in early December 1882, New Madrid County court judges ordered construction of fireproof vaults. They planned to use monies collected from back taxes.[85]

Chapter 9

Courthouse Square Park

After the New Madrid courthouse burned in 1905, several surrounding towns, including Lilbourn, sought the title of county seat. Landowners stood by, willing to donate land for a courthouse site. Cities consider a courthouse an important prize for their citizens.

In early November 1912, New Madrid County Treasurer Shapley R. Hunter Jr. certified that $20,000 "was in his hands" for building a new courthouse, provided that the voters authorize the issuance of bonds at a special election. The other stipulations were that "it be authorized within eighteen months, and the removal of the county seat to Lilbourn is defeated at the election of November 5, 1912." Citizens guaranteeing the certificate were A. B. Hunter, Lee C. Phillips, David Mann, H.E. Broughton, Murray Phillips, T.H. Digges, Thomas Gallivan, and Dr. George Dawson.[86]

Residents of nearby Lilbourn believed its location would guarantee that it become the county seat. It was located on the "best" rail lines junctions. The name "Courthouse Square Park" survived in Lilbourn for a while, but the county seat remained in New Madrid. Long-time Lilbourn resident Harold Ponder wondered if Lilbourn's current generation had ever heard of its "Courthouse Square Park."[87]

In a hot countywide election in the fall of 1912, voters rejected a bid for the courthouse by the city of Lilbourn.[88]

A year later, in November 1913, a group of citizens signed a pledge that the $20,000 would be used if the issuance of bonds were approved at a special election of December 3, 1913.[89] Lilbourn wanted to be the seat of justice and managed to prevent bond issues from being voted in while waging a legal battle that ended in the Missouri State Supreme Court.

In early April 1914, New Madrid's counsel, Col. Tom Gallivan, traveled to Jefferson City to file an application in the Supreme Court for a "writ of mandamus" on State Auditor Gordon. New Madrid County had recently issued $50,000 in bonds for constructing a courthouse and jail. Gallivan's mandate was to register the $50,000 in bonds with Gordon. New Madrid's other counsel, Judge Henry Clay Riley, and his son, Harry Boone Riley, along with Gallivan, won the county's case.[90] The Supreme Court of the State of Missouri disposed of the case by determining that,

"The bonds had been duly authorized and they should be registered. Let our peremptory writ go. All concur." [91]

On July 11, the *Weekly Record* announced that the courthouse question had been settled. The editor congratulated the people of New Madrid County on the permanent location of the county seat, and pontificated as follows:

"The time has come when there is no longer any rivalry between New Madrid and Lilbourn as to which shall have the courthouse, and good sense dictates that the people of both towns should get together in promoting the prosperity of our whole county.

"The city of Lilbourn is a fine place and has a bunch of the most active and progressive business men in Southeast Missouri. They made a long and gallant fight for the county seat under adverse conditions, and would have won should such a thing have been possible. They never lost heart or admitted for a moment that they might not win. Everything was done to capture the prize.

"New Madrid's growth and development has been hampered by the long and bitter contest with Lilbourn, and investors have been made timid, notwithstanding the prominence of this city in the Mississippi Valley for 125 years, and its place in early history under the French and Spaniards.

"The Supreme Court has decided the bonds valid, and the fight is over." [92]

Before the new courthouse was built, an enterprising photographer climbed the city water tower and took a panoramic snapshot of Main Street. The large site (next to the old Richards Undertaking Company) where the courthouse burned in 1905 is bare. However, in the distance, the river and sandbar are in view. The 1916 levee had yet to be built. Today a view of the river is obscured by the levee.

Chapter 10

Construction Delays

In the spring of 1914, residents had voted bonds for a new courthouse,[93] and a sketch of the building soon appeared in the hometown newspaper.[94] From architectural plans submitted, the court selected those of a St. Louisian, H.G. Clymer. Clymer later designed an Art Deco building in Carondelet (St. Louis) that would become a Coca-Cola syrup plant.[95] Clymer's courthouse drawings called for a brick, stone-trimmed building, 107 by 75 feet. The court also accepted Interstate Building and Construction Company's bid of $80,000 for the shell.

It has been said that every key government building in the United States, from the late 1700s through the Franklin D. Roosevelt administration, was consecrated in a Masonic courthouse laying ceremony.[96]

The date was set. The New Madrid courthouse cornerstone ceremony would be Independence Day, 1916. The night before, an honored guest who was "one of the most famous Masons in the Mississippi Valley, and past pastor of the Southern Methodist Church in New Madrid for half a century," arrived in town. Rev. Dr. C.C. Woods held a reception at the Fairfield Hotel to greet the "present generation" of New Madrid people. Later in the evening, Masonic brethren greeted the Grand Master of Missouri Masons, Frank B. Jesse of Webster Groves.[97]

Chapter 10: Construction Delays

On the Fourth of July, at 1 p.m., the Masons processed from the Masonic Hall (located at the corner of Mott Street and Powell Avenue) to the courthouse site "south of the Opera House." Captain C.M. Barnes of Marston, grand marshal, led the procession and was joined by the Hon. H.C. Riley and Hon. William Dawson, grand deacons; Rev. Dr. Hawkins of Charleston and F.D. Kimes, chaplains; as well as three past worshipful masters: Sam Pikey, Point Pleasant Lodge 176, W.H. Copeland, New Madrid Lodge 429, and Louis Theilmann. Joining them were Wood and Jesse and Clymer, as well as Grand Junior Warden Charles D. Knott. A brass band set the tone and led the procession to the unfinished courthouse, where officers sat on a covered platform. The brass band was likely New Madrid's Silver Band, at one time made up of sixteen local musicians.[98]

A building's cornerstone is the foundation stone, and generally the first stone set in the construction of a masonry building. Subsequent stones are set in reference to this stone. Over time, a cornerstone evolved into a ceremonial masonry stone or replica, set in a prominent spot on the outside of a building. Inscriptions vary, but generally include construction dates and the names of architects, builders, or other significant persons. The New Madrid 1916 ceremony was almost identical to the one used by our country's first President, George Washington (also a Mason), when the cornerstone of the capitol building was laid in 1783.

Using Masonic tools—the square, level, and plumb—Grand Master Jesse declared that the stone was found to be square, level, and plumb, and then proclaimed,

> "The craftsmen have done their duty. I find that the craftsmen have skillfully and faithfully performed their duty, and I declare the stone to be well-framed, true and trusty, and correctly laid according to the rules of our ancient craft."

After Deputy Grand Master Virgil P. Adams of Hayti poured corn on the stone, Senior Grand Warden S.J. Smalley poured wine on the stone, invoking Divine blessings. Jesse then added,

> "Protect the workmen against any accident, long preserve the structure from decay, and grant to all of us a supply of the corn for nourishment, the wind of refreshment, and the oil of joy. Amen."

A copper box was inserted with the cornerstone in the northeast corner of the building. The box held copies of "all the New Madrid County papers and St. Louis papers, and carefully prepared historical events, including names of those who contributed the $20,000, names of all county officers, etc." [99]

In early 1917, additional funds were authorized for the courthouse and jail, but by then, the threat of World War I had reduced the labor force, so no bids were received.[100]

Chapter 11

A Well Deserved Dedication

Finally, in 1919, the courthouse interior was finished under the leadership of master builder W.W. Taylor of Cape Girardeau. Final costs exceeded $100,000.[101]

A 1919 photo shows four rows of men, dressed in suits and holding hats, standing at attention on the east steps of the nearly completed courthouse. At the rear, a few females decked out in hats can be seen. Riley Bock located the original photo in his uncle's collection in Charleston, Missouri. While a comprehensive list of those who have been identified appears in the photo caption, the names of many from this distinguished group have been lost to history. Two rows back is "a somber-faced, white-headed and bearded L.A. [Lilbourn Anexamander][102] Lewis, who had fought hard to move the county seat and build the courthouse in his newly-established town of Lilbourn." He had lost, but "there he is celebrating the day." [103]

In 1898, Judge Henry Clay Riley had begun the effort to build a new courthouse, and he was with the effort to the end. A notation in his ledger book survives: "Court House burned September 2, 1905." During the Lilbourn-New Madrid contest for the courthouse location, he played a key role in the bond litigation at the State Supreme Court in 1914.

In June 1922, in an unprecedented move, two ladies—Mary Meatte of Portageville and Laura Jackson Winston of New Madrid—filed for the August Democrat primary election for recorder of deeds.[104] The Woman Suffrage Act was ratified in August 1920. That October the League of Women Voters sponsored a mock election which County Chairman Mrs. A.O. Cook said was to "give women an opportunity to learn the actual methods of casting ballots." [105]

Returning to the first ladies to file for election two years later, evidently, Winston withdrew before the primary election, which Meatte subsequently lost. In September, the Republican Central Committee selected the full county ticket, among whom was Peter Smith for recorder.[106] Democrat Shapley Hunter, Jr. won the election, took office, and began his duties January 1, 1923.[107]

Then, in 1926, citizens elected the first female to serve in county office: Lillian Dawson as circuit clerk. Dawson had served as deputy under her father, William Dawson, Sr.[108] She was the last family member to reside in the historic Hunter-Dawson home before it was sold to the city in 1966,[109] and later transferred to the State of Missouri for a state park.

In 1933 and 1934, Mrs. John Moylan served as assessor, perhaps taking on the position held by her husband John, who served from 1932 to 1933.[110] Her given name has been lost to history.

In later years, several women have served as county office holders. After the death of Recorder George Boone in 1983, his deputy, Doris Hampton, ran the office for a period of time. Ann Evans Copeland served as deputy recorder of deeds for twenty-five to thirty years, followed by a stretch as recorder of deeds.[111] Mary Margaret Phillips Brown served as probate clerk in the 1960s. Jane Ellen Nunn and Nancy Pardon served as public administrators, as does today's Paula Scobey.[112] Currently, Marsha Holiman fills the role of circuit clerk, Tracy Barnes serves as probate clerk, and Amy Preyer is an assistant prosecuting attorney. Kim St. Mary Hall is recorder of deeds.

Chapter 12

Our Officials' Finest Hour

Perhaps the finest hour to grace our courthouse occurred in January 1937, when officials opened its doors to citizens in crisis, including me. Serious flooding from the Mississippi River not only threatened the city of New Madrid, but also brought a constant stream of refugees to town. Some had been evacuated from the Birds Point Spillway area east and north of town and others, from the floodway district north of Portageville. Others converging on the courthouse were Civilian Conservation Corps (CCC) and Works Progress Administration (WPA) laborers, the American Red Cross, and a few townspeople, including my family and me. During the flood scare, we had not been able to leave town. My father, Arthur Shy, had to stay close to our dairy farm: he could not abandon his twelve Guernseys and Holsteins, which had to be milked twice a day. In addition, his customers who stayed in town depended on his door-to-door milk delivery, and my family needed the income.

In January 1937, men in "great numbers" descended on New Madrid to help save the levee under the direction of the U.S. Army Corps of Engineers. The WPA and CCC, along with the Red Cross, found temporary quarters in the courthouse. Although the Red Cross is not a government agency, it can be counted on to provide shelter, food, health, and mental health services during a disaster. To feed the more than 1,500 laborers assigned for flood fighting duty, the CCC set up a kitchen in the courthouse basement.

The Missouri Relief Commission sent commodities, which were also stored in the courthouse. Included were 752 sacks of flour, 1,000 pounds of fresh beef, and 200 pounds of salt pork to feed the distressed. In addition, the headquarters at the courthouse received 2,000 pieces of clothing and bedding.[113]

When the river stage at New Madrid reached 43.5, the Corps of Engineers sent all available personnel from Memphis and Vicksburg to New Madrid, where they first set up temporary offices in the old Commercial Hotel. Both the upper Mississippi and the Ohio rivers poured their waters into the giant Mississippi at Cairo, Illinois. This is when the Corps ordered the evacuation of the Spillway area, and about 500 families of refugees were brought to the courthouse in New Madrid. Red Cross employees and volunteers worked night and day to process refugees so the CCC trucks could take them to Sikeston, where they were housed and fed.[114]

After the Corps warned that the mainline levee could break, New Madrid residents scaffolded their furniture, and many left town to seek shelter with relatives or friends who lived on higher ground. Merchants placed fixtures and stock on eight- to ten-foot-high scaffolds, or else moved them to a higher floor, and boarded up front show windows that would have been vulnerable to floating logs or debris. The hometown newspaper, the *Weekly Record*, reported that practically every business in town, with the exception of two bars and the hotels, closed.

My grandparents, Probate Judge Lee C. and Neelie Waters Phillips, were among anxious townspeople who gathered valuables and left town, tackling icy Highway 61 north to St. Louis to find shelter with a son. To supplement her husband's salary as a judge, Neelie raised concord grapes and cotton with the help of her handyman, Lige Byrd. She also raised chickens and sold eggs, so before evacuating, she locked her chickens in a henhouse with

Chapter 12: Our Officials' Finest Hour

a chain, asked her nephew Dick Mott to keep an eye on them, and hoped for the best. Neelie was a strong and resourceful woman whose ancestors were pioneers who had come to New Madrid in the late 1700s and early 1800s. They, along with other New Madrid people, had waited out many an "overflow." But this time was different, and as she and my grandfather headed to St. Louis, she worried about leaving her daughter Mildred (my mother), her son-in-law Arthur and the grandchildren, but she knew they couldn't leave town because of the demands of their dairy farm.

The difference this time was that just ten years before, in 1927, the new mainline levee had failed at Dorena. Floodwaters surrounded the courthouse and destroyed many structures in the city. In those days, there was no Birds Point-New Madrid Floodway and no setback levee. It was said that nearly all of New Madrid County was under water in 1927, except for a small, fairly dry part of the eastern half.[115] Memories of scrambling ahead of the levee break and later scrubbing out mud and debris from homes and businesses were still fresh in townspeople's minds.

In the meantime, Judge Phillips, in his sixth year as probate judge, made arrangements—should the situation get worse—for his daughter Mildred and her family to move into the probate judge chambers on the first floor of the courthouse. My family's farm lay southwest of town—about where Cargill's is located today—in a very precarious situation between the mainline levee and the river. So, sometime during the frigid night of January 23, my parents Arthur and Mildred faced a hard choice and made the decision to abandon their home. According to my grandmother's diary,[116] "Mildred and the children expedited to the courthouse." My mother would always say,

> "Listening to the sound of chunks of the river bank falling into the river that night was eerie."

As the situation worsened, at around 9 p.m. my parents awakened everyone and, with sleet pelting from all sides, crammed seven children (along with basic food and clothing) into their 1936 Chevrolet sedan and headed for the courthouse. I was seven years old and don't recall being afraid, but the grownups surely feared they would never see their home on the river again. The days of hearing the calliope whistle as the riverboats drew closer, and the nights of sitting on the front porch cooling off with river breezes might soon vanish. Not to mention the real threat to the vital outbuildings and my father's livelihood—his herd of dairy cattle.

Remembering my family climbing the slippery steps to the first floor of the courthouse, I can still recall seeing scared and weary refugees from the Spillway area, holding on to their tired and whining children. They were lined up under the rotunda, awaiting transportation to nearby towns for higher ground and food and shelter. My sisters and I probably felt a little superior, because we were allowed to stay in the courthouse, but, in reality, we were refugees from the river, too.

After settling down in the probate court, my family discovered that entering and leaving our quarters required stepping gingerly over exhausted laborers. These hardworking men had been commandeered to sandbag levees. Sandbagging was a difficult job, as workers filled burlap bags with dirt and boards, and then hauled the heavy load to the levee top. WPA relief workers and local recruits slept on the cold, tiled courthouse floor at all hours. Mildred kept a close watch over her brood as she prepared meals for us on a kerosene cook stove, under less than ideal conditions. However, the big warm coal furnace of the courthouse was an unaccustomed luxury. For us as children, it was all a big adventure, partly because we were country kids now living in the city, and in the biggest building in town, no less.

I don't know how my mother did it, living in cramped quarters for three weeks. My older St. Louis cousins always said Mildred

Chapter 12: Our Officials' Finest Hour

Phillips was spoiled—her mother stitched her lingerie by hand—and well she could have been. Not only was she the baby of the family but the only girl with seven brothers. So, when she married my father, Arthur Shy, moving into the life of a dairy, cotton and corn farmer had to have been a jolt. But she had pluck, contending with setting hens and cantankerous roosters, and harvesting and canning from our fruit orchard and vegetable garden. With some "help" coming in by the day, she made a delightful home for us "down on the river." Sewing our dresses—some from flour sacks—on her treadle Singer machine, she sorted out siblings' squabbles over who was going to sit closest to the Philco radio to listen to "Little Orphan Annie" or "Amos Andy." In addition, she played the pump organ at the Immaculate Conception Church in New Madrid, showing up every Friday afternoon at our school for choir practice and every Sunday morning and daily during Lent for Mass. For sixty years she led the choir with her organ or until she could no longer negotiate the stairs to the choir loft.

Suddenly leaving her home on the river for the confined courthouse quarters had to have been a dreadful time for her. She was caring for all of us, including my six-week-old brother Robert, and creatively cooking three times a day with what few pots and pans she had managed to bring from her home. I know she missed her cast iron cook stove. But she had a great sense of humor. One night, my other brother, toddler Arthur, threw his glass milk bottle onto the courthouse floor. That white, hexangular-tiled floor was made to last—today it is still intact and beautiful after 100 years. The bottle shattered, and that was it. As my mother always said, "Arthur was weaned overnight."

As we busied ourselves with playing in the courthouse and visiting other relatives in town, my parents did what was necessary to keep us safe. My father "refrigerated" his bottled milk outside on the window ledges. Several mornings he awoke to find them gone, so he started leaving the windows partially open to detect the sound of the petty thief. It didn't happen again: as my oldest sister Josephine Shy Richardson said, "Everyone in town knew that Arthur J. Shy had a shotgun, and he knew how to use it." [117]

After a few weeks, with the flood scare over, we left the courthouse but my family never returned to the house on the riverbank. This episode of living in my grandfather's courthouse chambers was unforgettable, and one reason I chose to write this book.

Chapter 13

Disaster on the Mississippi

But horrors beyond my family's trials, too sad to speak of, were to come. Sometime during our prolonged stay in the courthouse, a barge on the river carrying workers back to New Madrid from the Birds Point Spillway sank. Thirty men, mostly young, drowned. Next door to the courthouse was the Richards Undertaking Company, where bodies awaited identification by families. In addition to frozen bodies of WPA workers were those of men from the surrounding countryside. It was said that "they were stacked up like cordwood." Many had heard the appeal for workers on the radio, and had left their families and heating stoves to save the levees. Times were hard. The Great Depression had left scores of men jobless, and many grabbed at a chance to make a little money.

Perhaps someday New Madrid will erect a memorial to honor these brave men. The following is a list of those drowned or missing as published in the February 5, 1937 issue of the *Weekly Record*: Clyde Scott, Charles Williams, C.J. Baker, Earl Ballard, William Smith, Bob Matthews, W.S. Tyler of Wardell; Jeff Baker, Frank Dean and Frank Lambert of Catron; Frank Dunlap, Matthews; William Dawson, New Madrid; M.L. Masters, Kennett; Luther Swingord, Orvile Hindman, and Jake Schlossen of Bell City; Steve Gibbs and Buck Smith of Ardeola; Charles Woodfin and Loman Lafe of Advance; and Don Pruitt, Harry Sanders and

Albert Neal of Bloomfield.[118] In addition, William F. Ruffin of Portageville also drowned.

On Monday, February 8, a week after the tragedy, a jury sat in the circuit court room for three hours during a formal inquest over the body of William F. Ruffin, one of the twenty-six workers who lost their lives on the sinking barge. Four men were still missing.

Serving on the all-male jury were Morris Frankle, a ginner; F.L. Steele, county supervisor; W.P. Hunter, levee contractor; Byron Stanley, son of Sheriff A.F. Stanley; H.B. Henderson, state liquor inspector; and Lennie Fontaine, barber shop owner, all of New Madrid.[119]

Coroner L.A. Richards said the inquest was to serve as a test case, and the verdict would hold on all other victims. The courtroom was filled to capacity, and the outside corridor was jammed.[120] Richards had ordered the inquest after government officials from the motorboat faulted the men for crowding the barge in their haste to get back to New Madrid for food and sleep. The men, in turn, blamed the government for overloading the barge. Prosecuting Attorney Conran questioned fourteen witnesses, among whom were several who had escaped to safety.

The jury's verdict blamed the inefficiency of the organization in charge—due to the emergency flood situation, the setup of the foremen was "hurried and inadequate." In turn, victims were held responsible for crowding onto the barge when they should have known it was overloaded.

Asked by the *Weekly Record* for his opinion of the verdict, Coroner Richards said, "I think the verdict was just. As far as I am concerned, the case is now closed." When the paper asked for Prosecutor J.V. Conran's opinion, he responded,

> "From the evidence as given by the witnesses the jury reached the only verdict that could have been reached. There will be no further investigation into the matter." [121]

Chapter 13: Disaster on the Mississippi

In mid-February, U.S. Congressman Orville Zimmerman, a Democrat two years into his role, announced that the WPA had advised him that river employees losing their lives would be considered as government employees, coming under the compensation laws, and that families and relatives of each drowned man would receive up to $3,500. The author could not verify that families were ever compensated.

Congressman Zimmerman, dissatisfied with the February 8 inquest, was quoted in a "Washington dispatch" saying there should be further investigation of the tragedy, and that the War Department "ought to be able to establish the cause of the accident 'more definitely.'" In the same report, the War Department said,

> "The War Department does not believe that any of the employees of the government can be directly charged with responsibility of this accident with all the circumstances and conditions taken into consideration." [122]

Photos

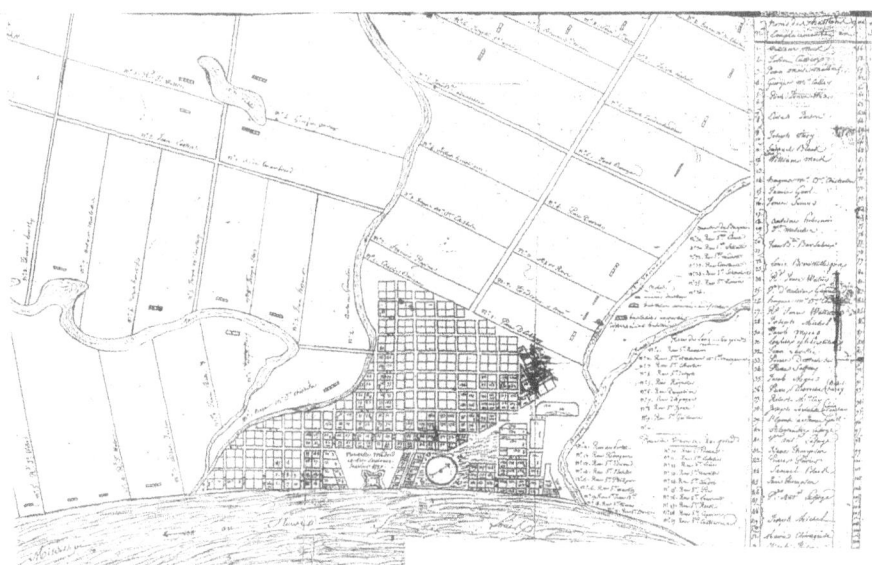

New Madrid Archives, Missouri Historical Society, St. Louis.

1794 Plat of Nouvelle Madrid showing Fort Céleste as indicated by the four-pointed star overlooking the river.

Floyd Calvin Shoemaker, *Missouri & Missourians,* Chicago: Lewis Publishing, 1943

American Log House on the Frontier - Sketch by Collot, 1826.

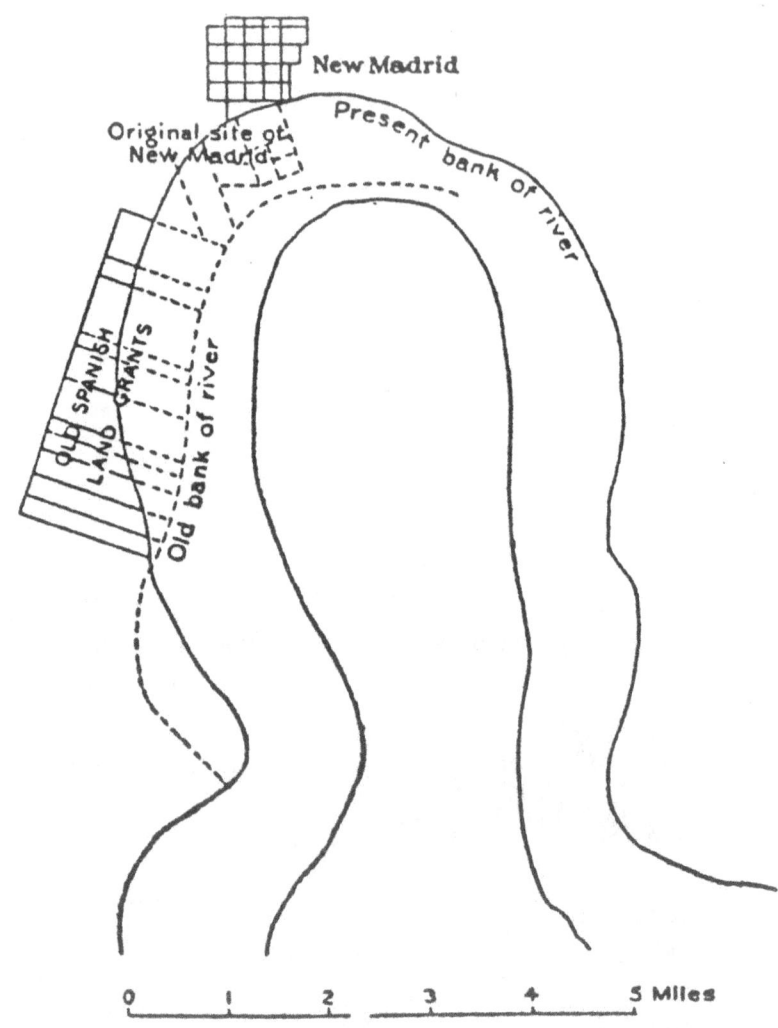

USGS, Washington, D.C.: U.S. Government Printing Office, 1912

The original location of New Madrid and Mississippi River bank in 1811 compared with the town site and river bank circa 1912.

Harper's Weekly 1871

1854 courthouse, built on lots 47 and 48 of the "County Addition," is the frame building with a porch on far right. Waterfront scene as sketched in 1871 by A.R. Waud.

County Court Deeds for 1823 County Addition to City of New Madrid

Lots 1 – 8 and 61-68. Deeded back to Prudence Peyroux on 4/3/1824. Peyroux had previously deeded the entire addition tract to the County Court. Prudence was the widow of Henri Peyroux, post commander from 1799 to 1803. After resigning, Henri relinquished his America property to Prudence and returned to France where he had numerous possessions.

Lot	Deed Book/Page	To
9	13/67	Ella D. Walling
10	13/20	Cyrenus Emmons
11	13/16	Alps. Delaroderie
12	13/207	Godfrey LeSieur
13-14	13/144	Richard Phillips
15	13/69	Nelson D. Walling
16	13/86	Jared Lee
17-18	13/92	Tho. Phillips
19-20	13/51	Jas. Russell
21	14/131	Pierre Jouter
22	13/20	Cyrenus Emmons
23-24	13/18	A. Audibert
25	12/131	George Netherson
26	13/63	Wm. L. Hiatt
27	14/378	Thos C. Powell
28	13/15	Robert G. Watson
29-30	13/23	Matteo Bigliolo
31-32	13/31	Mores Shelby (Recital)
33-34	13/16	Alps. Delaroderie
35-36	13/194	Joseph Crensier (Sp?)
37-38	13/31	Nelson D. Walling
39-40	13/16	Alps. Delaroderie
41	13/31	Nelson D. Walling
42		
43	12/156	James Evans (Recital)
44	13/81	Alp. Delaroderie
45-46	13/22	Geo. G. Alford
47-48	12/19	Frs St. Mary
49-50	17/16	Andrew Gilboney
51		
52		
53-54	17/190	Generieve Latourette
55		
56		
57-60	13/23	Matteo Bigliolo

History of Southeast Missouri, Chicago: Goodspeed Publishing, p. 300. Deed records extracted by H. Riley Bock.

Compiled by H. Riley Bock

List of initial lot sales in the "County Court Addition" of 1823 for the 1854 courthouse.

Photos

Dixie Riley Bock Collection, H. Riley Bock

New Madrid Banking Company, occupied by County Clerk Lee C. Phillips after the 1905 fire – the right side became Dawson Grocery and the left, the Post Office.

Jack C. Long Collection, H. Riley Bock

Peoples Bank—occupied by Probate Judge J.H. Bishop, Collector H.E. Broughton, and Sheriff T.F. Henry after the 1905 fire.

Photos

H. Riley Bock Collection

Newsum Bros. Grocery Store, corner of Main and Mott Streets, subsequently occupied by Kroger and then by Phillips Hardware—at the desk is Carrie "Toy" LaVallee, and one of the Newsum brothers is behind the counter.

Jack C. Long Collection, H. Riley Bock

View of the city of New Madrid with river and sandbar in background, taken from the water tower—the vacant lot next to Richards Undertaking Company is the site where courthouse burned in 1905 and was rebuilt in 1915.

Photos

Circuit Judge Henry Clay Riley, Sr.
1850-1920 – photo circa 1910.

Dixie Riley Bock Collection, H. Riley Bock

Dixie Riley Bock Collection, H. Riley Bock

H.C. Riley law office, Main Street, location of today's
Weekly Record next to old City Hall
Left to right: Judge Henry Clay Riley, Sr., Henry Clay
"Harry Boone" Riley, Jr. and unknown

Photos

Dixie Riley Bock Collection, H. Riley Bock

1919 courthouse officials and staff on front steps:
Front row: Ben Pikey, unknown, Frank Deane, Howard Riley, three unknowns, Fred Tickell, Circuit Judge Sterling H. McCarty, Henry Clay "Harry Boone" Riley, Jr., Former Circuit Judge H.C. Riley, Sr., James Finch, Mr. McKay, Col. T.J. Gallivan, J. Val Baker, Charles Shellenberger, John Randolph.
Middle Row: Jeff Adams, six unknowns, George Neumann, Will E. Davis, Moses Franklin, O.A. Cook, George H. Travlor, E.F. Sharp, Bob Ward, Richard Baynes, Otto Ankersheil, unknown.
Back Row: Three unknowns, F.M. Robbins, Shap R. Hunter, Jr., C.C. Bock, W.R. Rossiter, unknown, A.O. Allen, Marshall Alexander, A.B. Hunter, unknown, L.A. Lewis, unknown, Earnest Lagrotto, Frank Pierce, William Smith, Wes Sherwood, Louis Shields, three unknowns, T.F. Henry, Richard Pikey and Hillary Boone.

Martha Henry Hunter Collection, H. Riley Bock

New Madrid County Jai—former site of 1854 courthouse after it was moved from collapsing river banks. In use from 1919 to 1979 when replaced by a modern jail on Courthouse Square.

Photos

Harriet Shy Porter Collection

Probate Court Judge Lee C. Phillips
1859-1941
Photo, 1933.

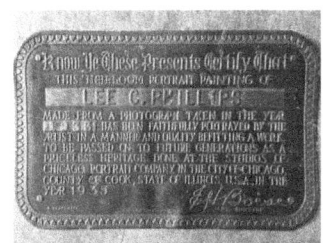

Harriet Shy Porter Collection

Judge Phillips heirloom portrait certification
1935 – Chicago Portrait Company
(attached to the back of the framed original.)

Mary Sue Anton

Weekly Record archives

Courthouse in 1937—view of north entrance from William "Bud" Dawson, Jr. filling station.

Photos

Ben & Vera Ashley Collection, Jane Ashley Vann

1947-48 Courthouse officials and staff (identifications are uncertain)

Front Row, left to right: Reba Jackson, Doris Hampton,
J.W. Daugherty, Rosannah Stanley Rodman,
Mary "Frog" Hunter Green, Felix Robbins,
Albert Ransburgh, Hartzel Kimes.
Middle Row: Erie Wright, Mary Margaret Brown, O.R. Rhodes,
unidentified, Bernard DeLisle, Hal E. Hunter, Jr.,
Miles R. Davis, Val Perkins.
Back Row: Agnes Newsum, Bert Femmer, Jess Wilkins,
Chester Ferguson, J.V. Conran, unidentified.

Patty Porter Frye, photographer

Courthouse today – view of east entrance.

Photos

Beth Papasakelariou, photographer

Centennial banner.

Patty Porter Frye, photographer

Second floor—mezzanine below Rotunda view
with centennial banner.

Beth Papasakelariou, photographer

Courthouse stained-glass dome.

Beth Papasakelariou, photographer

Circuit court chair flanked by U.S. flag, Missouri flag and the Great Seal of the State of Missouri on wall.

Photos

Patty Porter Frye, photographer

Probate court with Great Seal of the State of Missouri in background.

Beth Papasakelariou, photographer

New Madrid County Seal of 1821 over Prosecutor's office.

Photos

Andrew Lawson Collection

Leonardo da Vinci *The Last Supper* print miraculously salvaged after an arson home fire.

Beth Papasakelariou, photographer

Commemorative Centennial Christmas Ornament.

Photos

Ed Thomason, Photographer, *Weekly Record*

Centennial Committtee Members

Back-Left to Right: Sarah Fowler Ezell, Aaron Griffin, Lynn H. Bock, Ronnie Simmons, Larry Rost.
Front-Left to Right: Riley Bock, Edward Riley, Marsha Holiman, Paula Scobey.

Front Cover: Stack of court books archived in attic, including books used by Judge Lee C. Phillips

Patty Porter Frye, photographer

Chapter 14

The Workings of the County

Many government employees work inside the courthouse every day, and many other people pass through its doors on official business. Elected officials, appointed officials, county employees, state employees, lawyers, citizens and others with legal interests are in the courthouse in their various capacities. But what really goes on?

Attorneys: Most of the attorneys who practice law in New Madrid County are intimately familiar with the courthouse building and the staff. Attorneys represent clients in all types of legal matters, and they often work in the courthouse. In the movies and on television, we see the glamorous images of big-city law firms with posh offices and squads of good-looking lawyers, secretaries and paralegals in all kinds of dramatic situations. The life of a small town lawyer may not have the jet-setting glamour, and the day-to-day work may not be so dramatic, but the theme of helping people in need is very real. Attorneys are prepared by training and education to represent people in court, in both civil and criminal matters, and they are motivated by the desire to help their clients. They work closely with judges, prosecutors, opposing counsel, and courthouse staff to pursue justice and safeguard the rights of citizens.

Law practice in a small town or rural area requires the attorney to be well versed in a variety of legal issues. A lawyer in New Madrid might be called on to draft a will, handle a divorce, interpret a contract or defend someone who is accused of a crime. No doubt the lawyers who have practiced in the New Madrid courthouse over the years have encountered many difficult and heartbreaking situations as well as routine matters. Whatever the legal issue, the lawyer is sworn by an official oath to uphold the law and follow rules of professional conduct. The lawyer is a counselor, advisor, advocate and officer of the court, sworn to conduct himself with dignity and to respect the courts.

The citizens of New Madrid County are fortunate to have several attorneys in private practice available to advise them and guide them through legal issues. Other than lawyers who are currently county officials, the following New Madrid attorneys have active law licenses in the state of Missouri: H. Riley Bock, Lynn H. Bock, Charles C. Hatley, Hal E. Hunter, III, Hal E. Hunter, IV, Lawrence H. Rost, Brandon M. Sanchez, and Charles L. Spitler. These attorneys work under stringent ethical and professional rules and are required to have constant continuing legal education.

For those citizens who can't afford to hire a lawyer in criminal matters, a public defender may be appointed by the judge. The Missouri Bar in Jefferson City maintains a program of volunteer lawyers to assist needy persons, and the state maintains a free Missouri Seniors' Legal Helpline.

County Commission Clerk: In January 2004, then Governor Bob Holden appointed Clement Cravens as county clerk following the retirement of Jim Farrenburg. Citizens elected Cravens for his first full four-year term in November 2006, and re-elected him in 2010 and 2014.

Cravens explains that his duties are primarily divided into two areas—financial/budget and elections. His office handles payroll,

Chapter 14: The Workings of the County

vendor payments, the distribution of certain funds to various other political subdivisions—i.e. schools and cities—processing the tax rates for the county's political subdivisions, and conducting all elections within the county.

As owner of the *Weekly Record* newspaper and commercial print shop when Governor Holden appointed him in 2004, Cravens had experience in elections from printing the ballots for the county and reporting on the ballot tabulation every election night. He also published the annual financial statement for the county, so he had a basic knowledge of how the county operated financially. Still, admits Cravens, "It was a major learning process for me as a new county clerk."

Cravens enjoys all of the various duties of his job. He qualifies this with,

> "My least favorite time is on election day waiting for the polls to close—the longest day on earth!"

Within a month of being sworn in, the county clerk had to file for the election for the remaining two years on the unexpired term. Cravens continues,

> "Elected county officials are always nervous during an election's filing period, wondering if they are going to get an opponent; so as a "newbie" to my office, I was extremely nervous on the last day of filing.
>
> "My friend Bobby Hedgepeth—owner of Richards Funeral Home and a former county recorder and county commissioner—dreamed up a practical joke to play on me. As the final few minutes of the filing period ticked away, Bobby obtained copies of some blank filing documents and came into my office to notify me that he had filed for county clerk. With a straight face—while holding the

filing documents where I could see them so I would believe that he had actually filed—he explained that filing against me was nothing personal, but that he needed a few more years of service as a county official for a full retirement benefit, and running against a new office holder would be an easier election to win. Then he turned and walked out into the main office area, and when I came out behind him, the office was full of people who immediately broke into applause and laughter. I have to admit I was pretty astounded initially, but knowing Bobby and his history of shenanigans, I suspected something was up. To this day, he still relishes reminding me of the day he 'got me good.' " [123]

County Collector: Dewayne Nowlin serves as county collector. In 1997, Governor Mel Carnahan appointed Nowlin, then chief deputy collector, to fill out the term of Dub Scobey, who was retiring. He was elected to the office of county collector in 1998. Nowlin, a Gideon native, says he had tired of the corporate world, where he served as a sales representative for Philip Morris.

Nowlin's job is to collect taxes—personal property, real estate, railroad, and utility taxes. He enjoys working with the taxpayer, especially getting to know the people.[124]

In 1882, after county court judges ordered construction of fireproof vaults for the New Madrid courthouse, Collector Richard J. Waters notified citizens on the delinquent list that their property would be seized and sold for unpaid 1881 taxes.[125] Earlier that fall, Waters set up tax collection points in businesses as a convenience to taxpayers. It appears that no neighborhood was overlooked. A person could pay at R.M. Purdy's Store, New Madrid; Mott Davis & Company's Store, Point Pleasant; DeLisle Brothers Store, Portageville; Canoy's school house and Emory school house, Big Prairie; Mike Cook's, West Swamp; Little River Station; the school house in East Township, and the school house in St. John's Township.[126]

Chapter 14: The Workings of the County

County Assessor: Ronnie Simmons began work in the assessor's office in March 1982, and was chief appraiser for Assessor Clyde M. Hawes for many years. He was elected as assessor in 1996, and took office September 1997. The county assessor serves a four-year term, and is elected by the county at large. Unlike other local elected officials, whose terms begin the first day of January following the November election, the assessor is elected during the general election, but does not take office until the first day of September of the following year.

The office is located in the basement of the courthouse. The assessor is responsible for developing and maintaining a current list of all taxable real and tangible personal property in New Madrid County. The assessor is also responsible for assessing the property annually. Assessed valuation provides the tax base for property taxes levied by the county and its various political subdivisions. The assessor's office processes the county citizens' annual tangible personal property declarations for the next tax billing cycle. The assessor also performs tax mapping by maintaining and updating property lines based upon warranty deeds received from the New Madrid County recorder of deeds.[127]

Charlie Ice, whose father Bill Ice served in the surveyor position for thirty years, was the New Madrid County surveyor from 1972 to 2008. Charlie says his father resigned so that he himself could run for the office. However, on the last day of filing, Bill filed for office—a ploy mainly to make Charlie get out and meet people. Then, just before the election, Bill got worried that his son might not win, so he started campaigning for Charlie. Both names were on the ballot, so basically they ran against each other—a story that received much coverage and made all the Missouri newspapers. In the end, Charlie won.[128] Charlie currently serves as the Floodplain Administrator. He handles the GIS (geographic information system), mapping, deed work, and flood permits.[129]

Returning to New Madrid's beginnings, in 1789, its founder, George Morgan, brought three 'gentlemen' surveyors with him from Pennsylvania: Col. Israel Shreve, Peter Light, and Col. Christopher Hays. It was said that Morgan outlined the manner in which the surveys should be made that was thought to be far superior to that of Congress. A.J. Dawson wrote to Gov. Beverly Randolph of Virginia that, "The system of rectangular survey applied to public lands adopted in the following year by the government of the United States in the territory northwest of the Ohio, it would seem was really first devised by him [Morgan]." [130]

Courthouse Amenities: Former County Clerk Jim Farrenburg says the elevator, which took the place of an old stairwell, was installed in the early 1990s. Heat and cooling is provided in window units by a gravity-type, reverse cycle heater/air conditioner. The first ones were installed in the mid- to late 1960s.[131] Early on, a coal furnace heated the courthouse.

To those who worked in the courthouse before the Civil Rights Act of 1964, some memories are distressing. In the 1950s, restrooms and water fountains still carried "Whites Only" signs. Should a black person need facilities at the courthouse, he or she had to crawl through an open basement window that led to the janitor's quarters. The Civil Rights Act was, even then, a decade away.

County Treasurer: Steve Riley's first term as county treasurer began on New Year's Day 2013, and ran until December 31, 2014. He is now into the first year of his second term, which ends December 31, 2018.

His duties include receipting in the monies that the county receives. He then records the checks and automatic drafts completed in the county clerk's office. At the end of the month, his numbers and those of County Clerk Cravens must match. Riley

Chapter 14: The Workings of the County

says the county currently uses thirty-five funds. Five to six funds have quite a few entries each month; the rest are utilized on and off throughout the year.

The treasurer has an accounting degree from Southeast Missouri State University, and says that what he likes most is working with numbers. "It is good when the numbers match, but when they don't, I have to figure out why not, which can be challenging at times."

Riley likes his office location in the basement, as it is quiet.

He tells the story of one of his predecessors being appointed to the office in the 1970s:

> "The man had helped someone who was running for office, and needless to say, he didn't know much about his duties. As it turned out, the county commission had to hire a former treasurer to clean up behind him." [132]

Recorder of Deeds: Kim St. Mary Hall is into her second term as recorder of deeds, after serving as deputy since 1977. In her office, deeds are recorded, marriage licenses may be obtained, and military discharges are recorded. Other recordings are for Missouri tax liens or releases, Internal Revenue tax liens or releases, home school filings, and plats and surveys.[133]

The recorder's office could be the first courthouse office that young people encounter as they apply for a marriage license. After the wedding has occurred, the license is returned to the office and recorded. When newlyweds discover they need proof of name change for the license bureau or Social Security office, they can return to the recorder's office and purchase a certified copy of the marriage license.

Our servicemen may have their military discharges recorded here, where a copy may be requested. There is no charge for either service.

Other traffic in the recorder's office includes abstractors, who research records for individuals purchasing or refinancing a home or other real estate. Others looking for copies of deeds are banks, attorneys, realtors, and individual landowners.

All records are public except military documents, which became non-public following the terrorist action that felled the twin towers in New York City on 9/11/2001.

Hall's office is steeped in history. The deed records date from January 11, 1805, when David D. Wentzell of the "District of New Madrid in Louisiana" purchased a tract of land from Eli Pettibone of the same place. Wentzell paid $100 for the 200 acres "lying and being situated in the District of New Madrid aforesaid and on Bayou St. John." The acreage adjoined a tract of land belonging to Thomas Powers. Just three years before, on March 6, 1802, Pettibone had been granted this piece of land by His Most Catholic Majesty the King of Spain, or by his commissioned Commandant, Don Henri Peyroux.[134] By the spring of 1791, 219 settlers had taken the oath of allegiance to the King of Spain.[135]

The recording of marriage records dates from 1847, and unless noted, the participants are from New Madrid County. Alfred Delaroderie served as marriage clerk, and his first entry is as follows:

> "Joseph R. Neal to Marthena Brown on Wednesday, September 15, 1847 by Thomas J.O. Morrison, Justice of Peace. Recorded September 17, 1847." [136]

There are other instances of marriages performed before September 15 that year, but Joseph and Marthena's is the first marriage recorded at the courthouse, or at least the first extant marriage record.

An 1806 faded document is probably the most worthy of note

Chapter 14: The Workings of the County

in the recorder's office. It contains toasts by judges and militia officials of the New Madrid District lavishly praising Secretary of State James Monroe and U.S. Minister to Paris Robert Livingston and others for bringing about the Louisiana Purchase.[137] This document may reflect how citizens of New Madrid, especially those of French or Spanish descent, eventually came to accept becoming Americans.

Records from April 28, 2003 to present can be viewed on a microfilm or microfiche viewer. Researchers looking for proceedings prior to April 2003 can consult old record books.

Speaking of records, when the United States was in the throes of the Great Depression, President Franklin Roosevelt established the Works Progress Administration (WPA). After the 1929 stock market crash, thousands of Americans were unemployed, and this program provided jobs to construction workers, as well as writers, artists, and musicians. Under the umbrella of the WPA, the Federal Writers Project was established to create a Historical Records Survey. Laura R. Jolley, senior manuscript specialist at SHSM Research Center, Columbia, writes,

> "The survey had two purposes: to list manuscripts, church records, and public records in county offices; and to locate, classify, and catalog all county and city records to make them more easily accessible. Field workers were dispatched to each county and the city of St. Louis to record information about the nature and content of records in county courthouses." [138]

Later, the reader will learn how many hours were spent copying courthouse records on a manual typewriter in the early 1950s. Picture then WPA Historical Records Survey writers in the 1930s copying faded manuscripts by longhand. Their role was to fan out throughout the state, spending hours in hot or chilly courthouses or churches.

Supervisors were based in St. Louis, and communications were slow and frustrating. In October 1937, a lady from Doniphan writes her supervisor: "I do not make enough money to go to the expense of hiring a car to go out in the country."[139] Some could not afford gasoline, and for others, buying stamps to correspond with supervisors created a hardship.

A Mr. P. Pigg spells out his aggravation about tracking down lost church records in Big Springs. After finally locating them with a Hermann, Missouri pastor, Mr. Pigg runs into a roadblock. He writes,

> "He gave me to understand that if I wanted to see his records or where they were kept, he would not let me, as there was no sense to it, that it was none of the Government['s] business." [140]

Still, today the only extant records of some counties and churches are preserved in the WPA Historical Records Survey.

Circuit Court Clerk: Marsha Holiman serves as circuit clerk of Judicial Circuit 34. Unlike most courthouse employees, the circuit clerk is a state employee. She is the appointing authority for all the clerks. She is responsible for maintaining complete and accurate records of the court, collecting, accounting for, and disbursing all monies paid into the court, and performing other duties to help the court.

Holiman came to work in 1986 as a county clerk. Her first term as circuit clerk began in 1998, and she is into her fifth term. She enjoys working with the public, and her office's policy is to help whoever comes to the "window." Holiman says,

> "I am a public servant; I have been elected to this position."

Chapter 14: The Workings of the County

The circuit clerk office tries to help whomever they can, but cannot give legal advice. If there is a conflict, they try to assist. Holiman says that the best part of her job is "helping a couple adopt a child, or someone applying for a passport." [141] The circuit clerk also handles divorce and court records. Another job is to select and summons jurors. Questionnaires are sent out to 300 people, and thirty-five to forty prospects are called in every four months.

Karen Horton, who worked in the courthouse from 1979 to 1986 for Circuit Court Clerk Van Sharp, says that in the old days, all the jurors were men. "There was a winding staircase that went from a door off the courtroom and wound up to the attic. This is where the sequestered jury slept on cots." [142] One can imagine the secrets stashed under the jurors' belts, along with perhaps a sandwich or two, as they negotiated the steep stairs. Some jurors were old and worn out, some young and hearty, some out of shape and others in fine form after picking cotton or baling hay.

The circuit clerk—or maybe the county official—with the longest tenure is John A. Mott, who served from 1862 to 1902. At that time, the circuit clerk also held the position of recorder of deeds, so Mott spent forty years overseeing both offices.[143] The Mott residence, a restored, two-story frame structure, sits at the corner of Main Street and Pinnell Lane.

Circuit and Presiding Judge of the 34th Judicial Circuit: The Honorable Fred W. Copeland is circuit and presiding judge of the 34th judicial circuit (Pemiscot and New Madrid Counties). The circuit courtroom is located on the second floor of the courthouse in New Madrid, where it has been since the courthouse was built 100 years ago. Copeland considers it very convenient and accessible to the public.

Hon. Copeland presides over Division I of the circuit court in each county. As such, he primarily presides over felony cases that are bound over from the Associate Division, civil cases in which the amount in controversy exceeds $25,000, and domestic relations matters. He is also the juvenile court judge in New Madrid County.

Brian Abbott has served as the chief juvenile officer since 1994, and his office is in Caruthersville in Pemiscot County. Abbott's chief deputy is Diedra Freeman, whose office is in the New Madrid County Courthouse.

According to Office of the State Courts Administration in Jefferson City,

> "These courts hear a variety of matters specific to the family, including juvenile matters related to delinquency, status, child abuse and neglect, and termination of parental rights. A wide variety of services, including counseling, mediation, parenting classes, and social services are provided . . . either through in-house programs or through referrals to other agencies." [144]

As presiding judge, Copeland is in charge of the administration of other various courts in the circuit, such as Division II and Division III of the state courts in each county, and all the various municipal courts located within the circuit. This primarily entails the assignment of a judge to a case or to a court when it is required.

Hon. Copeland was elected to a six-year term as circuit judge in the 34th Circuit in 1988, and he took office in January 1989. He was re-elected in 1994, 2000, 2006, and 2012. He received a B.S. and J.D. from the University of Missouri-Columbia, and was then involved in private practice in New Madrid. He served as associate circuit judge of New Madrid County from 1982-1988, and has been on the bench for over thirty-three years.

Judge Copeland's father, Missouri Rep. Gene Copeland, served in the Missouri House for thirty-eight years; "longer than any other legislator in state history." Rep. Copeland died in 2007.

Chapter 14: The Workings of the County

Today's lawmakers are limited to eight years in the House, so his tenure will likely never be matched.[145]

Copeland enjoys dealing with the attorneys and their clients. "After all these years, every day and every case is different and unique. On the other hand, dealing with the public can be difficult."

He explains that many people in domestic relations cases come into the courtroom with blinders on as to how their case should turn out. If they don't get what they want, they feel as if they have been somehow mistreated by the system. Also, most people believe that someone convicted of a crime should be punished, unless that individual is a family member or a friend. He concludes,

> "Being a judge is not a popularity contest." [146]

In the September 1920 circuit court term—just a year after the courthouse was completed—the docket listed fifty-five couples seeking a divorce. The *Weekly Record* editor writes,

> "There are as many men seeking separation from their 'better halves' as there are women seeking to be untied from the matrimonial noose .... If this keeps up, Reno, Nevada will have to take a back seat and yield New Madrid County as the 'Mecca' in which to be freed from a misfit marriage yoke."

The editor decided this number (fifty-five couples) to be an unusually large number for a county containing but 25,000 people.[147] Was it the men returning from the trenches of World War I and trying to settle down in peacetime? Was it the shapeless flapper dress, women smoking cigarettes, the sudden popularity of make-up, the Charleston?

Dr. Randy Olson, a postdoctoral researcher at the University of Pennsylvania, has analyzed marriages and divorces back to pre-1870. His source is CDC's National Center for Health Statistics database. He writes "that events like WWI, WWII, and the Great Depression had a significant impact on marriage and divorce rates." No surprise there, but what might catch the reader unaware is that divorce rates today are actually slightly down compared with the 1970s, '80s and '90s on a per capita basis. The cause is partially due to marriage rates declining steadily since the 1980s. Today they are lower than any other time since 1870, including during the Great Depression.[148]

Returning to the circuit court, the court holds a law day on the second and fourth Tuesday of each month. Terms of Court are in January, May, and September.

In September 2015, New Madrid County implemented electronic filing. Attorneys with cases in those courts that have put electronic filing into practice must use the Missouri e-filing System.

Associate Circuit Court Judge: The associate circuit court judge is Josh Underwood, who also presides over the probate division. Judge Underwood is into his first term, having succeeded Judge Charles L. Spitler. Probate is the "court procedure by which a will is proved to be valid or invalid." [149] All circuit courts have probate divisions that handle cases involving the estates of minors, of individuals who are unable because of incapacity or disability to manage their own estates, and of individuals who have died.[150] Digitized collections of court files are available online at the Missouri Secretary of State website. At this time, the collection includes New Madrid County Probate Court records from 1805 to 1830. These records include wills, administrator bonds, and estate inventories. Prior to 1866, the county court transacted probate business.[151]

Sometimes court officials perform duties outside the courthouse. I can recall my grandfather, Probate Judge Lee C. Phillips,

Chapter 14: The Workings of the County

greeting a prospective bride and groom in the late 1930s as they arrived one Saturday evening in an open Model T Ford—it could have been a Speedster—to say their vows at his home on Mitchell Avenue. Soon, amid much gaiety and laughter, their attendants followed them into the family's living room and witnessed the wedding.

Prosecuting Attorney: Andrew C. Lawson serves as the prosecuting attorney. According to the Missouri Association of Prosecuting Attorneys,

> "As the conscience of the community, the prosecutor is entrusted by the voters every four years to make decisions that protect the public.... Missouri's prosecutors are responsible for prosecuting misdemeanor and felony offenses that occur within their county. This includes representing the State at trial, probation violation hearings, and post-conviction hearings. Additionally, the prosecuting attorney represents the State in misdemeanor cases on appeal." [152]

Lawson's first term began January 1, 2015, and it expires December 31, 2018. He writes, "My day-to-day operations require me to serve as the chief law enforcement officer for New Madrid County. I am also the legal representative for New Madrid County on all civil matters."

Lawson is supported by Assistant Prosecuting Attorneys Lewis H. Recker and Amy M. Preyer. Lawson's experiences help him fulfill the role of prosecuting attorney. They are as follows:

August 2012-December 2014: New Madrid County Assistant Prosecuting Attorney.

November 2006-July 2012: High Intensity Drug Trafficking Area Prosecutor, United States Attorney's Office, Eastern District of Missouri.

May 2005-October 2006: Associate Counsel, Dempsey Law Firm, Washington, Missouri.

When asked what he likes most about his job, Lawson responds,

> "As cheesy as it sounds, I want to help people who are victims of crimes. I want to make the community I am raising my family in a safer place."

What Lawson likes least about his position is that the rules are in place to protect the constitutional rights of the accused at the expense of the victims.

His office is on the second floor of the courthouse, and he says the location "could be worse." He adds,

> "The public loves the 'idea' of an older courthouse such as New Madrid County's. However, from a practical standpoint, they are very inefficient. The space is limited for all of the countywide offices that are located inside the building, and security is always a concern."

He agrees that the countywide offices (all except the sheriff's department) are located under one roof for the convenience of the citizens. He then adds,

> "It would be nice to have the courthouse designated strictly for court purposes, but rarely is that the case." [153]

When quizzed about funny or sad stories, the prosecutor believes the funny ones would be appreciated only by those who appear in court on a daily basis, and not by the general public.

Chapter 14: The Workings of the County

"Unfortunately, there are far more sad stories to share when dealing with the criminal justice system. While I do my best to seek justice for victims, even if I am able to send the criminal to prison for the maximum amount of time allowed by law, the victims will still wake up the next day and continue to be victims of a crime.

"One example involved two families who lived out in the country next door to each other. These neighbors feuded for years. One night, one of the neighbors was arrested for driving while intoxicated, and he had the mistaken belief that his neighbor was the one who had turned him in. So he decided to wait until his neighbor and the neighbor's wife left town for the weekend, when he broke into their residence and completely burned it to the ground. The house that burned was more than just a house. It was a home. This family had lived in that house for thirty-nine years. They raised four children in that home, and stored every memory along the way inside. And, because their neighbor wanted revenge, he took it all away from them.

"The neighbor was arrested and convicted of burglary and arson, and sentenced to the maximum of fourteen years in the Missouri Department of Corrections. Sadly, that is little consolation to the family, who not only lost their shelter, but all their memories. But the reason I will always remember this case is because, when the family was sifting through the remains of their home, trying to find anything salvageable, they found the reproduction of da Vinci's *The Last Supper* that hung in their dining room for decades. It was completely burned except for Jesus in the middle. They told me that when they found this picture and saw the amazing way that it had burned, they felt a sense of relief, and knew everything was going to be all right."

Lawson adds, "I still get chills when I see this photo!" [154]

Sheriff: Terry Stevens serves as the county sheriff. His office is on the square across from the courthouse. Stevens' role as deputy sheriff began January 1, 1985, after he had started as a dispatcher. He first served as sheriff from January 1 to December 4, 1997, when he resigned "due to a charge of nepotism." During his absence as sheriff, Stevens worked as a special investigator for the prosecutor's office. After citizens re-elected him in 2000, he resumed the office in 2001, and has served ever since. It is an elective office every four years, in the same cycle as for the United States president.[155]

According to the Missouri Sheriffs' Association (MSA), a nonprofit organization founded in 1945, a sheriff is responsible for the safety and security of the judicial circuit court, as well as the transportation of prisoners between the courts and detention facilities. Stevens also serves court papers and eviction notices, and issues concealed carry permits and gun permits.[156]

Today, the New Madrid County jail is closed for renovations, so Sheriff Stevens transports his prisoners to Caruthersville.

It is difficult to visualize what made up a sheriff's day in pioneer times. Shoemaker writes that after the War of 1812, "Missouri was afflicted with a wave of lawlessness and crime so typical of the frontier. Criminals, gamblers, adventurers, and an objectionable squatter class came to Missouri." The pioneer was used to self-help in emergencies, so early Missourians often carried their guns and dirks with them. "All sorts of criminals seemed to choose Missouri as their sanctuary in this period, and when the law finally threatened to catch up with them, they would flee to Texas or Arkansas, other 'last stand' refugees of the criminals of the 1820s."[157]

The duties of today's sheriff may have changed over the years, but perhaps not to a great extent. In 1928, New Madrid County citizens signed a "Petition for Suppression of Vices," asking that "dance halls, gambling, dives, moonshiners and other sources of vice and annoyance" be suppressed.[158]

One of the last legal hangings in Missouri occurred in New Madrid in 1933. Two defendants involved in a botched robbery attempt pled guilty to murder without counsel during their first court appearance, and were sentenced less than a week later. The victim was twenty-seven-year-old grocery/gas station attendant Arthur Cashion, who was pumping gas at a station facing U.S. Highway 61, south of New Madrid. Circuit Judge John E. Duncan said, "I sentence you to die by hanging by the neck, until you are dead, dead, dead." [159] It was up to Sheriff Sam J. Harris to hang the two men from a scaffold after they robbed and murdered Cashion.[160] The Sheriff was quoted as saying,

> "It is going to be a very unpleasant duty for me to perform. I knew the duty when I asked the people of New Madrid County for the sheriff's office." [161]

In 2015, the MSA voted to install the United States national motto, "In God We Trust," on Missouri patrol vehicles. Sheriff Stevens says all decals were donated, and officers installed them at no cost to taxpayers.[162]

Coroner: George DeLisle's role as coroner is an elected position. He is into his first term, having taken office January 1, 2013. His office is located in Portageville.

In 1985, the Missouri Coroners' and Medical Examiners' Association was established for the benefit of members who are duly elected coroners in the state of Missouri. DeLisle's duties include investigating certain types of deaths, such as homicide, suicide, accidental, criminal abortions (including those self-induced), and child deaths (under age of ten). Other obligations include executing process when sheriff is disqualified, holding coroner's inquest or jury, or ordering an autopsy.[163]

The DeLisle family has been in the funeral business in Portageville for 115 plus years. As far as what experience DeLisle brought to this office, he says he has been a licensed embalmer and funeral director for thirty years. He worked for the New Madrid County Ambulance for twelve years as an emergency medical technician (EMT). He has been with the Portageville Fire & Rescue Department for thirty years, and currently serves as assistant chief. He is a Missouri State First Responder, and the past president of St. Eustachius school board. He also serves as a board member of the Portageville Housing Authority. He adds, "My past experience in all of these offices gave me the knowledge and experience to be able to run the office of coroner, and to be able to set up the office so it is accountable."

DeLisle adds, "It is very sad to make notification to any family that a loved one has died. The first Christmas I worked two fatal car accidents. When making notification at one family home, they already had the table set for their Christmas dinner. Having to tell them that they had just lost their loved one was extremely hard. I realized at that point that the coroner position would be the final voice for the deceased." [164]

Public Administrator: Public Administrator Paula Scobey writes that the public administrator is a court-appointed guardian of the individuals—and/or conservator of the estates of individuals—who have been declared incapacitated or disabled. A person can be incapacitated by reason of any physical or mental condition to receive and evaluate information or to communicate decisions. The result is a lack of capacity to meet essential requirements for food, clothing, shelter, safety, or other care such that serious physical injury, illness, or disease is likely to occur. The public admin-

Chapter 14: The Workings of the County

istrator serves as advocate for such individuals, as well as acts as conservator on behalf of minors of decedent estates. In addition to this office petitioning, it receives cases from social service agencies, or individuals, pending action and direction from the court.

Scobey followed H. Riley Bock as public administrator January 1, 2013, for a four-year term, after serving as probate division clerk for thirty years. She says that her office and the probate court work closely together, since the authority of her office comes from the probate court. She went into this position already having knowledge of the estates administered by the public administrator, as well as knowledge of probate.

The favorite part of her job is "helping others who cannot help themselves."

As the public administrator, Scobey is responsible for every aspect of her wards' care. This includes having to make life or death decisions based on documentation received from the wards' doctors, nurses, etc. She adds, "This is by far the most difficult part of this position." [165]

Early on, the New Madrid County Court began providing for orphaned children. Later, the jurisdiction transferred to the probate court. In the case of an orphan who was left with an estate, the court placed the child under the guardianship of some responsible citizen who entered into bond for the "safekeeping and proper management of the orphan and of the estate."[166]

If there were no estate or relatives, a child would be bound out as an apprentice—this has been going on in New Madrid County for over 200 years.

In early November 1814, Bernard Laffont [LaFont] gave a bond and signed an indenture to take on such an orphan. In the document, Laffont promises to teach the six-year-old male the art of farming, in addition to spelling, reading, and writing. The apprentice was to live with and serve Laffont until March 7, 1830, at which time the apprentice would be twenty-one years of age.[167]

Today's public administrator says that there is something new in the courthouse every day. She recalls the jokes played on individuals, and the "chaser" fireworks on the 3rd of July, "which wouldn't happen today."

Scobey closes her e-mail interview with,

> "The most important thing is from the past to the present, each office in the courthouse works together toward a common goal, which is to serve the public as best as we can." [168]

Chapter 15

Other Homes in the Courthouse

Over the years, many government agencies have found a home in the courthouse. I retain pleasant memories of my role as a secretary in the early fifties for the Farmers Home Administration, a Department of Agriculture agency located in the basement. I spent many hours in the recorder's office searching for deeds and other documents. I then transcribed them on a manual typewriter, using bond paper and onionskin to accommodate carbon paper for duplicates. People actually survived with no elevators, air conditioning, computers, scanners, printers, or smart phones.

On a particularly sweltering, stifling day, one of my bosses took two Emerson table fans home to provide relief to his family. The basement was fairly cool so the fans had been stashed in a storage closet. A day or so later, a Government Accountability Office (GAO) auditor arrived unannounced. My boss received a reprimand but he was mostly just embarrassed. Oh, if we had such oversight today.

The Farmers Home Administration (FmHA) was established in 1945 to replace the Farm Security Administration and, in 1994, its functions were transferred to the Farm Service Agency (FSA). In 2006, the FmHA was fully terminated.

Right around the corner at that time was the Missouri Extension Service. Next door was the Agricultural Stabilization and Conservation Service (ASC), another Department of Agriculture agency whose tasks are now carried out by the FSA.

License Bureau: Edna Riley Ellington, lifelong New Madrid resident, remembers that one of her first trips to the courthouse was in November 1955, to pick up a brochure to study for a driver's license test, written and driving. Today, the License Bureau is under state regulations, and is located in the basement. Every four years the office places a bid to continue. New drivers must obtain a Missouri learner's permit and then an intermediate driver's license before being issued a full Missouri driver's license. Today, in Missouri, formal classroom driver's education is not required.[169] The New Madrid agent is Terry Cole.[170]

Public Health Office: As early as June 1933, the Federal Emergency Relief Administration authorized the use of its funds for nursing, medical care, and emergency dental work. This was part of President Roosevelt's New Deal. New Madrid's public health office was located on the second floor of the courthouse, with Dr. William Neville O'Bannon in charge. Lorene Sides, who worked for the Extension Service, has lived in New Madrid most of her life. She remembers going to Dr. O'Bannon's office after school with her brother Raymond to hold out their arms for diphtheria and typhoid shots.[171] I recall Dr. O'Bannon and his staff appearing at the Catholic school and lining up students for immunizations. It was probably easier than rounding up the entire student body and keeping track of them as they marched across the street to the courthouse.

Today's New Madrid County Health Department was established in 1950. In 1995, after many years in the historic A.B. Hunter home on Main Street, the agency moved to Highway 61 under the leadership of Jayne Lewis Dees. Dees says the Main Street location did not have facilities to accommodate the disabled.[172]

School Superintendent Office: At one time, the county school superintendent's office was in the courthouse. Teachers took their tests there. After school integration the district became the New Madrid County R-1 Enlarged School District. Dr. Cynthia Sharp Amick of New Madrid is the superintendent and is the first woman in that position. Today this office and the Board of Education office are located on I-55 at the Howardville/New Madrid exit.

The Selective Service System: Selective Service had offices in the courthouse off and on for years. Selective Service was first instigated in 1917, after a "very slow enlistment following the U.S. declaration of war against Germany in April 1917." All males aged twenty-one to thirty were required to register for military service for a period of twelve months. Later, the age limit was raised to a maximum age of forty-five.

The Selective Training and Service Act of 1940 established the first peacetime conscription in United States history. All males between the ages of eighteen and sixty-five had to register. Following the December 1941 declarations of war against Japan and then against Germany, the service period was extended to last the duration of the war, plus a six-month service in the Organized Reserves.

Four Selective Service Acts have followed the first. Currently, Selective Service law refers specifically to "male persons." In early 2013, the Pentagon ended its policy of excluding women from combat positions. It was speculated that this would open the door for Congress to amend the law and remove the exemption from registration requirements.[173] Indeed, in December 2015, the Pentagon made a historic decision to allow women in all combat roles. This changed the constitutionality of an all male draft.

Clara Mitchell St. Mary was in charge of Selective Service on the courthouse's third floor, working as an agent. Jennie June St. Mary, who was related to Clara by marriage, also worked there from 1940 to 1945.[174] Kim St. Mary Hall says that when Clara's son and her father, Richard St. Mary Jr., came up for the draft in 1953, he enlisted in the Army so his mother wouldn't have to draft him.[175] Clara's daughter, Norma St. Mary Blankenship, says that later her brother, Herbert, also joined up voluntarily at Jefferson Barracks.[176] Today, Richard's daughter, Kim St. Mary Hall, is the recorder of deeds.

Red Cross: Libba Hunter Crisler was at the helm of the Red Cross located on the second floor. Her sister, Mary "Frog" Hunter Green worked alongside her. Dixie Baynes Leonberger says that her mother was among a group who met once a week during the war on the third floor to sew or knit mufflers, caps and socks for the military. They then packed and shipped them overseas. The project was under the sponsorship of the Red Cross.[177]

Abstractors: Jane Ashley Vann, manager of Security Abstract Company on Main Street, is not a public official, but has probably made as many trips to the courthouse as most employees. Vann's parents, Ben and Vera Ashley, worked for Merrill Spitler. Spitler, one of the few Republicans in New Madrid at the time, served as a Missouri representative in 1928.[178] Vann began working full time for her father in 1973 and, upon his death in 2001, took over as manager. Abstractors search records at the recorder's office for any tax liens filed against property owners, or if they need to view the "true" documents. They trace old surveys and plats with onionskin paper, a ruler, and a pencil. They then insert the copies in the abstracts of title being compiled. Abstractors also double-check the recorder's deed of trust records to assure they are not missing anything in their abstract records. Then they might go to the probate court to copy estates of someone in the chain of title who was deceased, to also show in the abstract.

Chapter 15: Other Homes in the Courthouse

Next, an abstractor checks for payment of taxes in the collector's office, and then takes a trip upstairs to the circuit clerk's office to check for judgments against property owners.

Vann recalls the times she had to go to the attic to search old records, and she admits it is much neater up there now than before.

She remembers that the recorder's office used a huge Xerox brand copy machine, maybe ten by four feet, and copies were processed through water and a big drum. When her father became recorder of deeds, people were amazed at how fast he could type on a manual typewriter. One of Ben Ashley's penchants was going out into the rotunda at around 4:45 each Friday and producing noises that sounded exactly like a train whistle. This meant he was leaving his office, as it was quitting time.[179]

Conclusion

By definition, courthouses are buildings where judges convene to adjudicate disputes and administer justice, but as described, they are much more. The New Madrid courthouse stands grandly in the center of town, signifying the dignity of the law and the services of the county government. The very building reminds each citizen of the precious freedoms and civil rights that are enshrined in American law. Today, in a handsome structure 100 years old, daily life—with all its drama and normalcy—goes on in the courthouse. As the centerpiece of a small American town, it is looked upon by many with affection and nostalgia. Duties may have changed insignificantly or drastically, but county officials still graciously perform their tasks for the people of New Madrid County.

Since I spent many hours in the courthouse as a child when my grandfather was probate judge in the 1930s, and later lived in the courthouse during the flood scare of 1937, I took on writing the history of the courthouse with zeal. The rewards were great as the fascinating story unfolded. The history of this great building is something every Missourian can be proud of and needs to be told, especially on the occasion of its centennial. Interviewing office holders was inspiring, as it became apparent that each ran for public office with the idea of serving the public and helping those in need.

Some citizens visit the courthouse on routine errands (such as recording a property transaction), others on exciting business (such as getting a marriage license), and still others on very serious matters (such as facing criminal charges), but all deserve respect and a comfortable and safe environment. And today, for citizens, researchers, visitors, defendants, and the lawyers who travel back and forth to their offices on Main Street or in the outlying county, the New Madrid County courthouse offers modern, pleasing, and well-designed quarters for whoever walks through its doors. No doubt this imposing building will continue to be of service, witnessing major events in the lives of the citizens of New Madrid County for a long time to come.

Acknowledgments

Since the inception of this book I have received help, encouragement and ideas from many people. Unlike while researching and writing my book, *New Madrid: A Mississippi River Town in History and Legend*, this time my dear husband Arthur Anton, M.D. was no longer with us. Since his death in 2014, I have greatly missed his faith in my writing, in addition to his support and humor.

I wish to thank my children for supporting me and cheering me on throughout this project: David Anton of Cortez, Colorado; Beth Anton Papasakelariou and her husband Cristo Papasakelariou, M.D. of Houston, Texas; and Philip Anton and his wife Yuriko of San Diego, California along with their children, Wyatt and Miles Anton of San Diego and Brace, Mari and Tristan Young of Cambridge, Massachusetts. Thanks also to David's daughter Marta Anton Soppe and her husband Ivan Soppe of Newberg, Oregon, and their daughter, Olivia Reese Soppe, plus a host of other friends and relatives across the country who gave me confidence to write yet another book.

Thanks also to my first family, Josephine (deceased) Shy Richardson, Harriet Shy Porter, Laura Neal Shy Sinex, Clare Shy Winter, Arthur Shy, Jr., Robert Lee Shy, Alice Shy Recker, Loretto Shy Alexander and Ruth Shy. Plus a host of nieces and nephews

Acknowledgements

and grand nieces and grand nephews, and cousins, all part of my large and loving extended family.

A special thanks to niece Patty Porter Frye and daughter Beth who served as photographers. Also Beth's constant support, generosity with her valuable time and legal knowledge, reading, editing, and encouragement every step of the way helped me reach for the skies and keep my eye on the ball.

I'd also like to thank my friend Kathy Braeuer of Seabrook, Texas, a fellow former Missourian, for just being there and whose support was much appreciated. My friend Carolyn O'Malley of Leawood, Kansas gave wise input on the title and Mary Radnofsky of Alexandria, Virginia who came in for tea one day and finished my bibliography.

A special thanks to local historian and attorney H. Riley Bock of New Madrid who supported me, graciously shared his scholarship and collections, and read the first draft of this book.

My first efforts spoke to the history of the courthouse with an original working title of *Evolution of a Courthouse: New Madrid County, Missouri*. Then, I thought my readers might want to know what actually takes place inside a courthouse, so I began interviewing current courthouse officials. They were all tolerant of my endless follow-up questions, and my prodding a few of them to get their answers back to me. I appreciate the stories these officials sent me—and their forgiveness of my lack of knowledge.

Thanks to Ed and Linda Thomason, publishers of New Madrid's *Weekly Record*, for assistance in locating and identifying old photos, and to my *Weekly Record* Facebook page friends, too numerous to list, who didn't hesitate to come forward with answers to my questions.

And thanks go out to other friends in New Madrid and the surrounding area, including Lorene Sides, Jan Farrenburg, Norma Jean St. Mary Blankenship (Cape Girardeau), Anna Lee Hayes, Dixie Baynes Leonberger, Martha Henry Hunter, Ann Evans Copeland, and Virginia Riley Carlson. All racked their brains to respond to questions about something that happened years ago.

I wish to recognize with thanks Rhonda Bickerstaff and her team at the New Madrid Memorial Library for their attention and assistance in accessing newspaper files.

And, finally, a special note of thanks to my publisher, Yolanda Ciolli, AKA-Publishing, Columbia, Missouri for her design expertise and for suggesting the current title while bringing this book to fruition. Thank you to my very talented editor Theresa Cameron, especially for eliminating my redundancies and run-ons.

All in all, this manuscript became a book in a very short time but only because of all of you.

Appendices

Endnotes

1   *Weekly Record,* 23 August 1902.

2   Judy Moore Bierman, telephone conversation with author, Elgin, IL, 27 October 2015.

3   Mildred Phillips Rhode, conversation with author, Zapata, TX, June 1993.

4   Dama Phillips Moore, conversation with author, Venice, FL, 02 July 1994.

5   J.A. Parker, Blytheville, AR, Eulogy at Judge Phillips' funeral, New Madrid, 18 May 1941.

6   *Weekly Record,* 17 June 1893.

7   *Weekly Record,* 4 July 1893.

8   *Southeast Missourian,* New Madrid, 09 January 1908.

9   J.A. Parker Eulogy.

10 Ibid.

11 Floyd Calvin Shoemaker, ed., *Missouri and Missourians: A Land of Contrasts and People of Achievements,* 5 vols., (Chicago: Lewis Publishing, 1943), 1:120.

12 Louis Houck, *Spanish Regime in Missouri: Collection of Papers and Documents Relating to Upper Mississippi*, 2 vols., (Chicago: R.R.Donnelley and Sons, 1909), 1:309.

13 Ibid, 1:319.

14 Ibid, 1:322.

15 Henry Peyroux Order, 03 July 1802, instru. no. 1055, New Madrid Archives, MHS.

16 *History of Southeast Missouri* (Chicago: Goodspeed Publishing, 1888), 482.

17 H. Riley Bock, "January 1919; The New Madrid County Courthouse," New Madrid County Courthouse, 1915-2015, 2015 Calendar, 1, (The *Weekly Record* LLC, 218 Main, New Madrid, MO.)

18 Ryan Eddy, County Executive Director, New Madrid Farm Service Agency, telephone interview by author, New Madrid, 24 July 2015.

19 "Plans are Underway to Mark the 100th Year of the County's Courthouse," *The Weekly Record* 149, no. 15, New Madrid, 11 April 2014.

20 Robert Shy and Alice Shy Recker, telephone conversations with author, Whitewater and Pleasant Hill, 31 October 2015.

21 *Weekly Record*, 12 Dec. 2014.

22 Goodspeed, 891-92.

23 Ibid, 437.

24 Ibid, 333.

25 Ibid, 301.

26 Goodspeed. 334, 35.

27 Robert Sidney Douglass, *History of Southeast Missouri: A Narrative Account of its Historical Progress, its Peoples, & Its Principal Interests,* 2 vols., *vol. 1, (Chicago & New York: The Lewis Publishing Company),* 1912, 242.

28 New Madrid County Court Orders, 1816-1825, February Term, 1822, 48, Reprint, T.C.L. Genealogy, Miami Beach, Fl., 1990. Viewed New Madrid Memorial Library, New Madrid, 24 October 2003.

29 New Madrid Co. Deed Book 2, 13 January 1808, 86-87 and Deed Book 4, 11 Mar. 1811, 185-86.

30 *Weekly Record*, 10 April 2015, no. 15.

31 Ibid, 06 February 2015, p. 8.

32 Louis Houck, *History of Missouri: From the Earliest Explorations and Settlements Until the Admission of the State into the Union, 3 vols., (Chicago: R.R.Donnelley and Sons), 1908,* 2:105-07.

33 Ibid.

34 Ibid, 2:279.

35 Agreements, Francois Riche Dupin and Louis Baby, 06 April 1802, instrument number 1040, New Madrid Archives, Missouri Historical Society, St. Louis.

36 Originally Upper Louisiana, so named by René Robert Cavalier de La Salle, referring to all lands drained by the Mississippi River.

37 Pierre Antoine LaForge, "Report to Gov. Carlos DeHault DeLassus, 1796."

38 Floyd Calvin Shoemaker, "New Madrid, Missouri, Mother of Southeast Missouri," *Missouri Historical Review* 49.4 July 1955; 324.

39 Floyd Calvin Shoemaker, Immaculate Conception Church Sesquicentennial address, 15 October 1939, New Madrid, MO. [*New Madrid Weekly Record,* 20 October 1939.]

40 H. Riley Bock, e-mail to author, New Madrid, 18 February 2015.

41 New Madrid Co. Court Orders, 1816-1825, May Term, 08 May 1821.

42 Shoemaker, *Missouri and Missourians*, 1:121.

43 Houck, *Missouri,* 1:118.

44 Goodspeed, 333.

45 Houck, *Missouri,* 2:143-44.

46 Ibid, 2:161.

47 Ibid, 2:144.

48 Douglass, 2:164.

49 Secretary of State, Missouri State Archives, Probate Records, s1.sos.mo.gov.

50   New Madrid Co. Record Book No. 5, 54-56.

51   Goodspeed, 327-28.

52   Ibid, 333.

53   New Madrid Co. Criminal Court Records, 1816 – 22 vols., vol. 1, 4.

54   Goodspeed, 328-29.

55   New Madrid Court Orders, 1816-1825, 33 vol., vol. A: 7.

56   Ibid, vol. A: 11.

57   Ibid, vol. A: 7, 11 and 21.

58   Winchester was named for Col. Henderson Winchester, who lived in the vicinity. (Douglass, *History of Southeast Missouri*, 1:291.)

59   New Madrid Court Orders, 1816-1825, vol. A: 34-35.

60   "New Madrid Notice: Sale Lots in the Town of New Madrid," Mark J. Stalcup [sic], John Shanks, and Thos. Bartlett, commissioners, *Jackson Independent Patriot*, 12 October 1822, SHSM.

61   Goodspeed, 329.

62   "Moved to Justice," H. Riley Bock Reflections, *Sikeston Standard Democrat*, 21 January 2014.

63   Goodspeed, 329.

64 "Moved to Justice," H. Riley Bock Reflections, *Sikeston Standard Democrat*, 21 January 2014.

65 *Weekly Record*, 30 September 1905.

66 "History of New Madrid's Street Names," part 1, Bock, *Weekly Record,* 20 November 1998.

67 A.R. Waud New Madrid County courthouse sketch *Harper's Weekly,* 1871.

68 "Moved to Justice," Bock, *Sikeston Standard Democrat*, 21 January 2014.

69 Bock, email to author, 21 October 2015, New Madrid.

70 *New Madrid Times*, 07 April 1860, SHSM.

71 The New Madrid County Courthouse 2015 Calendar, February and March.

72 New Madrid Co. Court Records, 33 vol., 1816, 1:379.

73 "Moved to Justice," H. Riley Bock Reflections, *Sikeston Standard Democrat*, 21 January 2014.

74 *Weekly Record*, 30 September 1905.

75 *Weekly Record*, 18 June 1904.

76 *Weekly Record*, 30 September 1905.

77 *Weekly Record*, 16 March 1907.

78 New Madrid's first city hall was built in 1904. (*WR*, 18 March 1966, 2:5.)

79 *Weekly Record*, 30 September 1905.

80 Goodspeed, 358.

81 Ibid, 322.

82 Ibid, 368.

83 Ibid, 370.

84 Ibid, 374.

85 *Weekly Record*, 16 December 1882.

86 "New Madrid's Offer to Pay $20,000 if Court House is Built in New Madrid," notarized 02 November 1914. *Weekly Record*, 09 November 1912.

87 Harold Ponder, telephone interview by author, Lilbourn, Missouri, March 2003.

88 *Weekly Record*, 21 November 1912.

89 *Weekly Record*, 22 November 1913. Pledge signers were A.B. Hunter, Lee Hunter, T.H. Digges, Jos. F. Gordon, T.J. Brown, D.O. Kimes, W.D. Knott, Chas. L. Proffit, D.R. Hunter, Wm. Dawson, Jr., Daniel Comfort, W.H. Garanflo, M.J. Conran, S.R. Hunter, Sr., H.C. Riley, Jr., W.O. Newsum, J.A. Hummel, Tom Gallivan, S. Manheimer, L.F. Lafont.

90 H. Riley Bock, "January 1919, The New Madrid Courthouse," New Madrid County Courthouse, 1915-2015, 2015 Calendar.

91 Reports of Cases Determined by the Supreme Court of Missouri between July 2 and July 14, 1914, Perry S. Rader, reporter, "State ex rel. New Madrid County et al v. John P. Gordon, state auditor, In Banc, 02 July 1914," vol. 260, April Term, 1914.

92 *Weekly Record*, 11 July 1914.

93 *Weekly Record*, 18 April 1914.

94 *Weekly Record*, 09 May 1914.

95 https://whatthatwas.files.wordpress.com/2014/02/img_0664.jpg. Accessed 09 November 2015.

96 En.wikipedia.org, Accessed 12 April 2015.

97 *Weekly Record*, 08 July 1916.

98 Ibid, 18 March 1966, 2:10. An undated photo caption identifies uniformed band members as Jim Shead, Leon Block, Tom Allen, Ed Heslinger, Gordon Cruchon, Fred Garanflo, William N. O'Bannon, Walter Meier, Albert Lee, Frank Pierce, George Garanflo, ___ Burns, John Long, Jack Martin, and Hunter Broughton.

99 *Weekly Record*, 08 July 1916.

100 *Weekly Record*, 13 January; 09 June; 07 July; 04 August 1917.

101 *Weekly Record*, 10 January 1919.

102 Inscription on tombstone at Evergreen Cemetery, New Madrid.

103 Bock, 2015 Calendar narrative, New Madrid County Courthouse, 1915-2015.

104 *Weekly Record,* 02 June 1922.

105 *Weekly Record,* 01 October 1920.

106 *Weekly Record,* 01 September 1922.

107 Recorder of Deeds, New Madrid.

108 *Weekly Record*, 18 Mar. 1966, Centennial Edition, Section 1, page 9.

109 *Weekly Record*, 17 August 1966.

110 "Officers of New Madrid District and County, WPA, Missouri Historical Survey, #779, 10 April 1939.

111 Ann Evans Copeland, telephone interview with author, New Madrid, 16 March 2015.

112 Jane Ashley Vann, e-mail to author, New Madrid, 05 August 2015.

113 *Weekly Record*, 29 January 1937.

114 Ibid.

115 "New Madrid Fights the Encroaching Mississippi," *St. Louis* (Missouri) *Post-Dispatch*, 22 April 1927.

116 Neelie Waters Phillips 1935-1944 diary, 23 January 1937, New Madrid, in possession of author.

117 Josephine Shy Richardson, email to author, Kokomo, IN., 27 September 2003.

118 *Weekly Record*, 5 February 1937.

119 *Weekly Record*, 12 February 1937.

120 Ibid.

121 Ibid.

122 Ibid, 19 February 1937.

123 Clement Cravens, e-mail to author, New Madrid, 21 April 2015.

124 Dewayne Nowlin, telephone interview with author, New Madrid, 22 September 2015.

125 *Weekly Record*, 16 December 1882.

126 *Weekly Record*, 21 October 1881.

127 Ronnie Simmons, e-mail to author, 10 April 2015; telephone interview with author, New Madrid, 10 August 2015.

128 Charlie Ice and Ronnie Simmons, telephone interview with author, New Madrid, 08 October 2015.

129 Simmons, interview with author, New Madrid, 08 September 2015.

130 J. Dawson to Gov. Beverly Randolph, "Virginia State Papers, vol. 4, p. 554-55, Richmond: no publisher given, 1795, as quoted in Houck, *Missouri,* 1:115-118.

131 Jim Farrenburg, telephone interview with author, New Madrid, 25 August 2015.

132 Steve Riley, e-mail to author, New Madrid, 11 April 2015.

133 Kim St. Mary Hall, fax to author, New Madrid, 19 March 2015.

134 New Madrid County Record Book, Book no. 1.

135 Pierre Antoine LaForge to Charles DeHault DeLassus, 31 Dec. 1796, New Madrid Archives, MHS.

136 New Madrid County, Missouri Marriage Records, 1847-1874, Book C, page 1.

137 New Madrid County Record Book, No. 1, Miscellaneous Deed Record 1:85, County Court Records, New Madrid.

138 Laura R. Jolley, "From the Stacks, Research Center—Columbia, Missouri in the Great Depression: The WPA Historical Records Survey Collection." *Missouri Historical Review*, 109:4 (July 2015), 269, SHSM, Columbia, MO.

139 Ibid.

140 Ibid, 270.

141 Marsha Holiman, telephone conversation with author, New Madrid, 04 April 2015.

142 Karen Horton, Sikeston, MO., *Weekly Record* Facebook page, 25 April 2015.

143 J.A. Barrett, "Officers of New Madrid County and District Have Been," Clerks Circuit Court and Recorders, #784, WPA, Historical Records Survey, New Madrid County Joint Manuscript Collection, 11 April 1939.

144 Office of the State Courts Administration, www.courts.mo.gov., accessed 27 August 2015.

145 Rudi Keller, "Former State Lawmaker Copeland Dies at 74," *Southeast Missourian*, 20 February 2007.

146 Hon. Fred Copeland, e-mail to author, New Madrid, 13 April 2015.

147 *Weekly Record*, 24 September 1920.

148 www.randalolson.com accessed 08 November 2015.

149 Henry Campbell Black, *Black's Law Dictionary*, 5th ed. (St. Paul, MN, West Publishing Col, 1979), 1081.

150 Office of State Courts Administrator, "Circuit Court Judges and Commissioners," Other Divisions, https:/www.courts.mo.gov., accessed 27 August 2015.

151 Barrett, WPA #792, Historical Records Survey, 10 April 1939.

152 Missouri Association of Prosecuting Attorneys, www.mo-prosecutors.gov., accessed 27 August 2015.

153 Prosecuting Attorney Andrew Lawson, e-mail to author, New Madrid, 15 September 2015.

154 Ibid.

155 Sheriff Terry Stevens, e-mail to author, New Madrid, 02 September 2015.

156 Missouri Sheriffs' Association, http://www.mosheriffs.com.

157 Shoemaker, *Missouri and Missourians,* 2 vols., 2:266.

158 H.A. Barrett, WPA #330 additional sheet, Historical Records Survey, New Madrid Co. MO, 05 December 1938.

159 *Weekly Record,* 26 January 1934.

160 *Weekly Record,* 29 December 1933.

161 *Weekly Record,* 26 January 1934.

162 *WR,* 21 August 2015.

163 Missouri Coroners' and Medical Examiners' Association, www.mcmea.org.

164 George DeLisle, e-mail to author, Portageville, 26 August 2015.

165 Paula Scobey, e-mail to author, New Madrid, 17 April 2015

166 WPA #8666, 28 May 1940.

167 Ibid.

168 Paula Scobey, e-mail to author, New Madrid, 17 April 2015.

169 Department of Motor Vehicles web site, dmv.org., accessed 01 Sept. 2015.

170 Fay Branum, License Bureau Office, telephone conversation with author, New Madrid, 30 October 2015.

171 Lorene Sides, telephone conversation with author, New Madrid, 30 September 2015.

172 Jayne Lewis Dees, telephone conversation with author, New Madrid, 01 October 2015.

173 https://en.wikipedia.org/wiki/Selective_Service_System, accessed 01 September 2015.

174 Karen Horton and Jennie Blankenship, *Weekly Record* Facebook pages, 09 March and 25 April 2015.

175 Kim St. Mary Hall, conversation with author, New Madrid, 07 September 2015.

176 Norma St. Mary Blankenship, telephone interview with author, Cape Girardeau, MO., 14 September 2015.

177 Dixie Baynes Leonberger, telephone interview with author, New Madrid, 09 November 2015.

178 www.S1.sos.mo.gov., accessed 14 August 2015.

179 Jane Ashley Vann, e-mail to author, 11 August 2015, New Madrid, MO.

Bibliography

Agreements, Francois Riche Dupin and Louis Baby. 06 Apr. 1802, instrument number 1040, New Madrid Archives, Missouri Historical Society, St. Louis.

Barrett, J.A. "Officers of New Madrid County and District Have Been—Clerks Circuit Court and Recorders," #784, WPA Historical Records Survey, New Madrid County, Joint Manuscript Collection, University of Missouri, Columbia, 10-11 April 1939.

Black, Henry Campbell. *Black's Law Dictionary*, 5th edition. St Paul, MN: West Publishing Co., 1979.

Bock, H. Riley. "Moved to Justice," *Reflections, Sikeston Standard Democrat*, 21 January 2014.

Bock, H. Riley. "January 1919; The New Madrid County Courthouse," *New Madrid County Courthouse Calendar*, 1915-2015.

Bock, H. Riley. "History of New Madrid's Street Names," part 1, *Weekly Record*, 30 October 1998.

Department of Motor Vehicles web site, dmv.org. Accessed 01 September 2015.

Douglass, Robert Sidney. *History of Southeast Missouri: Narrative Account of Its Historical Progress, Its People and Its Principal Interests*. 2 Vols. Chicago: Lewis Publishing Co., 1912.

Fuller, Myron L. "The New Madrid Earthquakes," USGS Bulletin 494, Washington, D.C.: U.S. Government Printing Office, 1912.

History of Southeast Missouri: Embracing a Historical Account of the Counties of Ste. Genevieve, St. Francois, Perry, Cape Girardeau, Bollinger, Madison, New Madrid, Pemiscot, Dunklin, Scott, Mississippi, Stoddard, Butler, Wayne and Iron. Chicago: Goodspeed Publishing Co., 1888.

Houck, Louis. *History of Missouri: From the Earliest Explorations and Settlements Until the Admission of the State into the Union.* 3 Vols. Chicago: R.R. Donnelley & Sons Co., 1908.

Houck, Louis. *Spanish Régime in Missouri: Collection of Papers and Documents Relating to Upper Mississippi.* 2 Vols. Chicago: R.R. Donnelley & Sons Co., 1909.

Jolley, Laura R., "From the Stacks, Research Center-Columbia, Missouri in the Great Depression: The WPA Historical Records Survey Collection," *Missouri Historical Review* 109.4 (July 2015): 268-71.

Keller, Rudi. "Former State Lawmaker Copeland Dies at 74," *Southeast Missourian*, Cape Girardeau, 20 February 2007.

LaForge, Pierre Antoine. "Report to Gov. Carlos DeHault DeLassus, 1796." *New Madrid Archives*, Missouri Historical Society, St. Louis.

Missouri Association of Prosecuting Attorneys, Missouri Coroners' and Medical Examiners' Association, www.mcmea.org. Accessed 15 August 2015.

Missouri Sheriffs' Association, http://www.mosheriffs.com. Accessed 27 August 2015.

Appendices: Bibliography

Missouri Supreme Court en banc. Reports of Cases Determined by the Supreme Court of Missouri between July 2 and July 14, 1914. Perry S. Rader, reporter. "State ex rel. New Madrid County et al v. John P. Gordon, state auditor, In Banc, 02 July 1914." Vol. 260, April term, 1914.

New Madrid County Court Orders, 1816-1825.

New Madrid County Criminal Court Records, 1816 – 22 vols., vol. 1, 4.

New Madrid County Deed Book 2. 13 January 1808, 86-87 and Deed Book 4, 11 March 1811, 185-86.

New Madrid County Marriage Records, 1847 – 1874.

New Madrid County Record Books, Book no. 1., No. 5.

"New Madrid Notice: Sale Lots in the Town of New Madrid," Mark J. Stalcup [sic], John Shanks, and Thos. Bartlett, commissioners, *Jackson Independent Patriot*, 12 October 1822, State Historical Society of Missouri.

"New Madrid's Offer to Pay $20,000 if Court House is built in New Madrid." Notarized 02 November 1914, *Weekly Record*, 9 November 1912.

"New Madrid Fights the Encroaching Mississippi," *St. Louis Post-Dispatch*. 22 April 1927.

New Madrid Times, 07 April 1860, State Historical Society of Missouri.

Office of State Courts Administrator. "Circuit Court Judges and Commissioners," Other Divisions, www.courts.mo.gov., accessed 27 August 2015.

"Officers of New Madrid District and County." *WPA Missouri Historical Survey*, #779, 10 April 1939.

Phillips, Neelie Waters. *Diary* 1935-1944, 23 January 1937, New Madrid, in possession of author.

"Plans are Underway to Mark the 100th Year of the County's Courthouse," *The Weekly Record* 149, no. 15, New Madrid, 11 April 2014.

Secretary of State. Missouri History: Missouri State Legislators, 1820-2000, Merrill Spitler, s1.sos.mo.gov. Accessed 14 August 2015.

Secretary of State. Missouri State Archives, Probate Records, s1.sos.mo.gov. Accessed 15 July 2015.

Selective Service System, http://www.sss.gov. Accessed 01 September 2015.

Shoemaker, Floyd Calvin. *Missouri and Missourians: A Land of Contrasts and People of Achievements*. Vols. 1 and 2. Chicago Lewis Publishing, 1943.

Shoemaker, Floyd Calvin, "New Madrid, Missouri, Mother of Southeast Missouri," *Missouri Historical Review*. 49.4 (July 1955): 317-27.

Virginia State Papers, vol. 4, Richmond.

Waud, A.R. New Madrid County courthouse sketch. *Harper's Weekly*, 1871.

Interviews/Facebook

Abbott, Brian. Telephone interview by author, Caruthersville, Missouri, 27 August 2015.

Bierman, Judy Moore, telephone conversation with author, Elgin, Illinois, 27 October 2015.

Blankenship, Norma St. Mary. Telephone interview by author, Cape Girardeau, Missouri, 14 September 2015.

Bock, H. Riley. E-mails to author, New Madrid, 18 February, 21 October 2015.

Branum, Fay. Telephone conversation with author, New Madrid, 30 October 2015.

Copeland, Ann Evans. Telephone conversation with author, New Madrid, 16 March 2015.

Copeland, Fred. E-mail to author, New Madrid, 13 April 2015.

Cravens, Clement. E-mail to author, New Madrid, 21 April 2015.

Dees, Jayne Lewis. Telephone conversation with author, New Madrid, 01 October 2015.

DeLisle, George. E-mail to author, Portageville, 26 August 2015.

Eddy, Ryan. Telephone interview with author, New Madrid, 24 July 2015.

Facebook, Inc. "*Weekly Record* Remember When in New Madrid," Jennie Blankenship, 03 September 2015. Accessed 04 September 2015.

Facebook, Inc. *"Weekly Record* Remember When in New Madrid," Karen Horton, Sikeston, Missouri, 25 April 2015. Accessed 01 May 2015.

Farrenburg, Jim. Telephone interview with author, New Madrid, 25 August 2015.

Hall, Kim St. Mary. Faxes to author, New Madrid, 19 March, 07 September 2015.

Holiman, Marsha. Telephone conversation with author, New Madrid, 04 April 2015.

Ice, Charlie. Telephone interview with author, New Madrid, 08 October 2015.

Lawson, Andrew. E-mail to author, New Madrid, 15 September 2015.

Leonberger, Dixie Baynes. Telephone interview with author, New Madrid, 09 November 2015.

Nowlin, Dewayne. Telephone interview with author, New Madrid, 22 September 2015.

Ponder, Harold. Telephone interview by author, Lilbourn, March 2003.

Richardson, Josephine Shy. Email to author, Kokomo, IN, 27 September 2003.

Riley, Steve. E-mail to author, New Madrid, 11 April 2015.

Scobey, Paula. E-mail to author, New Madrid, 17 April 2015.

Shy, Robert and Alice Shy Recker. Telephone conversations with author, 31 October 2015.

Sides, Lorene. Telephone conversation with author, New Madrid, 30 September 2015.

Simmons, Ronnie. E-mail to author, 10 April 2015; telephone interviews with author, New Madrid, 10 August 2015, 08 September 2015; interview with author, 08 September 2015

Stevens, Terry. E-mail to author, New Madrid, 02 September 2015.

Vann, Jane Ashley. E-mails to author, New Madrid, 05, 11 August 2015.

Index

Symbols

1794 Plat of Nouvelle Madrid, **39**
1821 county seal, **60**

A

Abbott, Brian, 76
abstractors, 72, 90
Adams, Jeff, **49**
Adams, Virgil P., 26
Agricultural Stabilization and Conservation Service, 87
Alexander, Marshall, **49**
Allen, A.O., **49**
American Red Cross, 29
Americans, 12, 73
Amoreaux, Michael, 13
Ankersheil, Otto, **49**
apprentice, 85
Arkansas, 8, 82
Ashley, Ben, 91
Ashley, Vera, 90
attorneys, 4, 65, 66, 72, 77, 78, 79

B

Baby, Louis, 8
Baker, C.J., 35
Baker, Jeff, 35
Baker, J. Val, **49**
Baker, Mark, 3
Ballard, Earl, 35
Barclay, Frank, 17
Barnes, C.M., 25
Barnes, Tracy, 28
Barry County, Mo., 8
Bartlett, Jesse, 13
Bartlett, Thomas, 15
Baynes, Richard, **49**
Bayouville, Mo., 14
Big Prairie, 13, 68
Birds Point-New Madrid Floodway, 31
Birds Point Spillway, 29
Bishop, J.H., 20, **44**
Blankenship, Norma St. Mary, 90
Bloomfield, Mo., 20, 36
Board of Education, 89
Bock, C.C., **49**
Bock, H. Riley, vi, 1, 66, 85, 95
Bock, Lynn H., 3, **63**, 66
Bollinger County, Mo., 8, 112
Boone, George, 28
Boone, Hillary, **49**
Bradley, Tom, 3
Broughton, H.E. [Henry E.], 20, 21, **44**
Brown, Amy, 3
Brown, Marthena, 72
Brown, Mary Margaret, **53**
Brown, Mary Margaret Phillips, 28
Building and Construction Company, 24
Butler County, Mo., 8, 20
Byrne, Napoleon "Nap" B., 18

C

Cairo, Ill., 30
Canoy's school house, 68
Cape Girardeau, Mo., 8, 27
Cargill's, 31
Carnahan, Governor Mel, 68
Carter County, Mo., 8
centennial:
  banner, 4, **55, 56**
  Christmas ornament, 4, **62**
  commemorative calendar, 4
  Committee, 3, 4, 5, 6, 10
  medallion, 4, 6
  portraits of founders, 4
Centennial, 10
Charleston, Mo., 25, 27

Index

child abuse, 76
Christian County, Mo., 8
civil cases, 76
Civilian Conservation Corps, 29, 30
Civil Rights Act, 70
Civil War, 18, 19, 20
Clark County, Mo., 8
Clymer, H.G., 24
Cole, Terry, 88
commandants, viii
Commercial Hotel, 30
Confederates, 18
Congress of the United States, 13
Conran, J.V., 3, 4, 36, **53**
conservator, 84
constitutional rights, 80
convention, west of the Mississippi, 12
Cook, Mrs. A.O., 28
Cook, O.A., **49**
Copeland, Ann Evans, 28
Copeland, Fred W., 75
Copeland, Gene, 76
Copeland, W.H., 25
coroner's inquest, 84
cotton, 1, 2, 30, 33, 75
County officials:
  Assessor, 5, 28, 69
  associate circuit judge, 76
  chief juvenile officer, 76
  Circuit Court and Presiding Judge, 75
  Circuit Court Clerk, 74, 75
  Commissioners, ii, 3, 5, 15
  Coroner, 36, 83, 84
  County Clerk, i, 20, 66, 67, 70, 74
  County Collector, 68
  County Health Department, 88
  County Treasurer, 17, 21, 70
  deputy juvenile officer, 76
  Floodplain Administrator, 69
  Justice of Peace, 72
  juvenile court judge, 76

  probate division clerk, 85
  Probate Judge, i, ii, 20, 30, 31, 78, 92
  Prosecuting Attorney, 3, 28, 36, 79
  Recorder of Deeds, 19, 28, 69, 71, 75, 90, 91
  Sheriff, 5, 13, 14, 19, 20, 36, 80, 82, 83
  surveyor, ii, 13, 69, 70
countywide offices, 80
Courthouse:
  1823 County Addition for, **42**
  1854 courthouse, 17, **41**, **42**, **50**
  Centennial, 2015, vi, viii, 3, 4, 5, 6, 10
  Cornerstone, 1919, 3, 27
  courtroom, 17, 36, 75, 77
  Dedication, 1916, 24, 25
  fire, 1905, 10, 19, 21, 23, 27, **43**, **44**, **46**
  stained-glass dome, 2, 4
  temporary quarters, 19, 29
  vaults, 19, 20, 68
Courthouse Square, **50**
Courthouse Square Park, 21
court records, ix, 13, 75, 78
Courts:
  Common Pleas/Quarter Sessions of the Peace, 12, 13
  family, 76
  Judicial Circuit 34, 74
  juvenile, 76
  law day, 78
  municipal, 76
  probate, i, ii, 20, 28, 30, 31, 32, 78, 85, 90, 92
  State, 76
  State Supreme Court, 22, 23, 27
Creek Indians, viii
Crisler, Libba Hunter, 90

D

Daugherty, J.W., **53**
Davis & Company's Store, 68

Davis, Greer W., 13
Davis, Miles R., **53**
Davis, Will E., **49**
Dawson, A.J., 70
Dawson, George, 21
Dawson Grocery, **43**
Dawson Jr., William "Bud", **52**
Dawson, Lillian, 28
Dawson, Robert D., 4
Dawson Sr., William, 28
Dawson, William (barge victim), 35
Day, Don, 3
Deane, Frank, **49**
Dean, Frank (barge victim), 35, **49**
death certificates, 2
declarations of war against Japan, 89
deed of trust records, 90
deed records, ix, 17, 72
Dees, Jayne Lewis, 88
defendants, 83, 93
DeLassus, Carlos DeHault, 8
DeLisle, Bernard, **53**
DeLisle Brothers Store, 68
DeLisle, George, 83
Democrat primary election, 27
Department of Agriculture, 87
Digges, T.H., 21
divorce, 66, 75, 77
dome, stained-glass, 2, **57**
domestic cases, 76, 77
Dorena, Mo., 31
Dorsey, Samuel, 13
Douglas County, Mo., 8
Douglass, Robert Sidney, 13
Dunklin County, Mo., 8, 20
Dunlap, Frank, 35
Dupin, Francois Riche, 8

E

earthquakes, 5, 13, 15
East Township, 68
Eddy, Ryan, 1
election, vii, 21, 22, 27, 66, 67, 68, 69

Ellington, Edna Riley, 88
emergency medical technician (EMT), 84
Emerson, David, 18
Emory school house, 68
estates, 78, 84, 85, 90
Ezell, Sarah, 3
Ezell, Sarah Fowler, **63**

F

Fairfield Hotel, 24
Farmers Home Administration (FmHA), 87
Farm Security Administration (FSA), 87
Farm Service Agency (FSA), 1, 87
Farrenburg, Jim, 66, 70
Federal Emergency Relief Administration, 88
Federal Writers Project, 73
felony offenses, 79
Femmer, Bert, **53**
Ferguson, Chester, **53**
Finch, James, **49**
Floods:
  1882, v, vi
  1927, 31
  1937, 29, 35, 92
Fontaine, Lennie, 36
Fort Céleste, viii, **39**
Foucher, Don Pedro, viii
Foucher, Pierre, 7
Frankle, Morris, 36
Franklin, Moses, **49**
Freeman, Diedra, 76
French, vii, 8, 12, 23, 73
French descent, vii, 12

G

Gallivan, Thomas, 21
Gallivan, T.J., **49**
Gibbs, Steve, 35
Gordon, State Auditor [John Pemberton], 22

Index

Gordon, William, 13
Government Accountability Office (GAO), 87
grand marshal, 25
Gray, William, 13
Great Depression, 35, 73, 78
Great Seal of the State of Missouri, 11, **58**, **59**
Greene County, Mo., 8
Green, Mary "Frog" Hunter, **53**
Griffin, Aaron, 3, **63**
Griffith, William, 19
guardian, 5, 84
gun permits, 82

H

Hall, Kim St. Mary, 90
Hampton, Doris, 28, **53**
hangings, 83
Harris, Sam J., 83
Harry S. Truman marker, **63**
Hatcher, R.H. [Richard H.], 17
Hatley, Charles C., 66
Hawes, Clyde M., 69
Hawkins, Rev. Dr., 25
Hays, Col. Christopher, 70
Hedgepeth, Bobby, 67
Henderson, H.B., 36
Henry Clay Riley, 27
Henry, T.F., **49**
Henry, Thomas F., 20, **44**
Hindman, Orvile, 35
His Catholic Majesty, viii
His Most Catholic Majesty the King of Spain, 72
Historical Records Survey, WPA, 73, 74
Holden, Governor Bob, 66
Holiman, Marsha, 3, 28, 74
homicide, 83
Horton, Karen, 75
Houck, Louis, 7
Howell County, Mo., 8

Hunter, A.B., **49**, 88
Hunter Bank Building, 19
Hunter-Dawson home, 28
Hunter III, Hal E., 66
Hunter IV, Hal E., 66
Hunter, Joseph, 13
Hunter Jr., Hal E., **53**
Hunter Jr., Shapley R., 21, 28
Hunter Jr., Shap R., **49**
Hunter, Lee, ii
Hunter, Timmie Lynn, 3
Hunter, W.P., 36
Hurley, Moses, 13

I

Ice, Bill, 69
Ice, Charlie, 69
Immaculate Conception Church, 33
indenture, 85
Independence Day, 24
"In God We Trust", 83
Internal Revenue tax liens, 71
Interstate Building and Construction Company, 24

J

Jackson, J.W., 19
Jackson, Reba, **53**
jail, 13, 15, 17, 18, 19, 22, 26, 82
Jasper County, Mo., 8
Jefferson City, Mo., 22, 66, 76
Jesse, Frank B., 24
Jolley, Laura R., 73
jurors, 75
Justice of Peace, 72
justices, 14
justice system, 2, 81

K

Kimes, Hartzel, **53**
Knott, Charles D., 25

L

Lafe, Loman, 35
LaForge, P.A. [Pierre Alexander], 13
Lagrotto, Earnest, **49**
Lambert, Frank, 35
L'Anse à la Graisse or Graisse, 7
LaVallee, Carrie "Toy", **45**
LaVallee, Don Juan, 8
LaVallee, John, 13
law, vii, viii, 2, 12, 37, 65, 81, 82, 89, 92
Law, 66, 79
law day, 78
Lawrence County, Mo., 8
League of Women Voters, 28
legislator, 76
Leonberger, Dixie Baynes, 90
LeSieur, Francois, 7, 15
LeSieur, Joseph, 7
levee, ii, 23, 29, 30, 31, 32, 35, 36
levee, mainline, 30, 31
Lewis, L.A. [Lilbourn Anexamander], 27, **49**
license bureau, 71, 88
Light, Peter, 70
Lilbourn, Mo., 21, 22, 23, 27
Little Prairie, 5
Little River Drainage District, ii
Livingston, Robert, 73
Louisiana Purchase, 8, 12, 73
Louisiana, Upper, 8

M

magistrates, vii
Malden, Mo., ii
Mann, David, 21
marriage, 2, 71, 72, 77, 90, 92
Masonic, 24, 25
Masonic Hall, 25
Masons, 24
Masters, Henry, 13
Masters, M.L., 35
Matthews, Bob, 35
McCarty, Sterling H., **49**
McDonald County, Mo., 8
McKay, Mr., **49**
Meatte, Mary, 27
Memphis, 30
microfiche viewer, 73
microfilm viewer, 73
Mike Cook's, 68
Military:
 discharge, 71
 Organized Reserves, 89
 overseas, 90
 peacetime conscription, 89
 service, 71, 76, 87
 women in combat roles, 89
Miró, Don Estevan, viii
misdemeanor offenses, 79
Mississippi County, Mo., 8
Mississippi River, v, 5, 9, 12, 16, 29, 30
Mississippi Valley, 23, 24
Missouri Association of Prosecuting Attorneys, 79
Missouri Coroners' and Medical Examiners' Association, 83
Missouri Department of Corrections, 81
Missouri driver's license, 88
Missouri e-filing System, 78
Missouri Extension Service, 87, 88
Missouri First Responder, 84
Missouri Historical Society (MHS), 8
Missouri learner's permit, 88
Missouri Relief Commission, 30
Missouri representative, 90
Missouri Sheriffs' Association (MSA), 82
Missouri State Supreme Court, 22, 27
Missouri Territory, 8
Monroe, James, 73
Morgan, George, 7, 12, 70
Morrison, Thomas J.O., 72
Morrison, T.J.O., 17

Index

Mott, Dick, 31
Mott, John A., 75
Moylan, John, 28
Moylan, Mrs. John, 28

N

National Center for Health Statistics, 77
Neal, Albert, 36
Neale, Thomas, 13
Neal, Joseph R., 72
Neumann, George, **49**
New Deal, 88
New Madrid archives, 8, **39**
New Madrid Banking Company, 20, **43**
New Madrid County:
　New Madrid County Ambulance, 84
　New Madrid County Health Department, 88
　New Madrid County School Superintendent, 89
New Madrid County Seal of 1821, **60**
New Madrid District, 8, 73
New Madrid Jail, **50**
New Orleans, viii, 7
Newsum, Agnes, **53**
Newsum Bros. Grocery Store, **45**
Newton County, Mo., 8
Nouvelle Madrid, **39**
Nowlin, Dewayne, 68
Nuevo Madrid, 7
Nunn, Jane Ellen, 28

O

O'Bannon, Dr. William Neville, 88
Ohio River, 30, 70
Olive, Jean Baptiste, 12
Oliver., Sen. R.B., ii
Olson, Randy, 77
Opera House, 25
Oregon County, Mo., 8

P

Pardon, Nancy, 28
parental rights, termination of, 76
Parker, J.A., i
pecans, ii
Pemiscot County, Mo., 8, 20
Pentagon, 89
Peoples Bank building, 20
Perkins, Val, **53**
Pettibone, Eli, 72
Peyroux, Don Henri, 8, 72
Peyroux, Henri, viii
Phillips Hardware, **45**
Phillips, Lee C., i, ii, 20, 21, **43**, **51**, 78
Phillips, Mildred, 31, 32, 33
Phillips, Murray, 21
Phillips, Neelie Waters, 30
Phillips, Samuel, 13
Pierce, Frank, **49**
Pigg, Mr. P., 74
Pikey, Ben, **49**
Pikey, Richard, **49**
Pikey, Sam, 25
Pink's Ice Cream Parlor, ii
pioneer, 31, 82
Point Pleasant, Mo., 25, 68
Ponder, Harold, 21
Portageville, Mo., ii, 27, 29, 36, 68, 83, 84
Portell, Tomas, viii
portraits of founders, 4
post office, **43**
Powers, Thomas, 72
Preyer, Amy M., 79
prisoners, 82
probate, i, ii, 20, 28, 30, 31, 32, 78, 85, 90, 92
Pruitt, Don, 35
Public Health Office, 88

R

Randolph, Gov. Beverly, 70
Randolph, John, **49**

Mary Sue Anton　　　　　　　　　　　　　　　　　　　　　　　　　　123

Ransburgh, Albert, **53**
realtors, 72
Recker, Alice Shy, 3
Recker, Lewis H., 79
Red Cross, 29, 30, 90
Reno, Nev., 77
Republican Central Committee, 28
Republicans, 90
Reynolds County, Mo., 8
Rhodes, O.R., **53**
Richards Funeral Home, 67
Richards, L.A., 36
Richardson, Josephine Shy, 34
Richards Undertaking Company, 23, 35
Riley, Ed, 3
Riley, Henry C., 20, **48**
Riley, Howard, **49**
Riley, Jr., Henry Clay "Harry Boone", 22, 27, **48, 49**
Riley, Sr., Henry Clay, 20, 22, 27, **48, 49**
Riley, Steve, 70
Ripley County, Mo., 8
R.M. Purdy's Store, 68
Robbins, Felix, **53**
Robbins, F.M., **49**
Rodman, Rosannah Stanley, **53**
Roosevelt, Franklin D., 24
Rossiter, W.R., **49**
Ross, Stephen, 5, 13
Rossville, Mo., 14, 15
Rost, Larry, 3, **63**
Rost, Lawrence H., 66
Ruddell, John, 15
Ruffin, William F., 36

S

Sanchez, Brandon M., 66
Sanders, Harry, 35
scaffold, 30, 83
Schlossen, Jake, 35
school integration, 89

Schultz, Christian, 17
Scobey, Dub, 68
Scobey, Paula, 3, 28, 30, **63**, 84
Scott, Clyde, 35
Scott County, Mo., 8, 14, 15
seat of justice, 13, 15, 22
Secretary of State, 73, 78
Security Abstract Company, 90
Selective Service law, 89
Selective Service System, 89
Selective Training and Service Act of 1940, 89
Shankle, W.O., 19
Shanks, John, 15
Shannon County, Mo., 8
Shapley Hunter, Jr., 28
Sharp, E.F., **49**
Sharp, Van, 75
Shellenberger, Charles, **49**
Sherwood, Wes, **49**
Shields, Louis, **49**
Shoemaker, Floyd Calvin, 9
Shreve, Col. Israel, 70
Shy, Arthur J., 29, 31, 33, 34
Shy, Jr., Arthur J., 33
Shy, Mildred Phillips. *See also* Phillips, Mildred
Shy, Robert, 3, 33
Shy's Pecan Orchard sundae, ii
Sides, Lorene, 88
Sides, Raymond, 88
Sikeston, Mo., 13, 30
Silver Band, 25
Simmons, Ronnie, 3, 5, 69
Smalley, S.J., 26
Smith, Buck, 35
Smith, Peter, 28
Smith, William (barge victim), 35
Smith, William (courthouse staff), **49**
Social Security office, 71
social services, 76
southeast Missouri, 1, 22, 71
Southern Methodist Church, 24

Spaniards, 7, 23
Spanish regime, viii
Spanish Royalty, 7
Spanish rule, 12
Spitler, Charles L., 66, 78
Spitler, Merrill, 90
Stallcup, Mark H., 15
Stanley, A.F., 36
Stanley, Byron, 36
State Courts Administration, Office of, 76
State Historical Society of Missouri (SHSM), 9
St. Charles, Mo., 8
Steele, F.L., 36
Ste. Genevieve, Mo., 8
Stevens, Terry, 82
St. Isidore Catholic Church, 8
St. John, Bayou, ii, 72
St. John's Township, 68
St. Louis, Mo., viii, 7, 8, 24, 26, 30, 31, 32, 73, 74
St. Mary, Clara Mitchell, 89
St. Mary, Jennie June, 89
St. Mary Jr., Richard, 90
Stoddard County, Mo., 8, 20
Stone County, Mo., 8
Story, Joseph, 13
suicide, 83
surveyor, ii, 13, 69, 70
survey, rectangular, 70
Swingord, Luther, 35

T

Taney County, Mo., 8
tax, 2, 19, 20, 67, 68, 69, 71, 83, 90
tax base, 69
tax liens, 71, 90
Taylor, W.W., 27
Terms of (Court), 78
Territorial Legislature, 8
Texas County, Mo., 8
Texas (state), 82

Theilmann, Louis, 25
Thomas, Richard S., 13, 14
Tickell, Fred, **49**
Travlor, George H., **49**
Trudeau, Zenon, viii
Truman, Harry S., 3
Twain, Mark, v, vi
Tyler, W.S., 35

U

Underwood, Josh, 78
Union soldiers, 18
University of Missouri-Columbia, 76
Upper Louisiana, 8
U.S. Army Corps of Engineers, 29
U.S. Congressman, 37
U.S. declaration of war against Germany, 89

V

Vann, Jane Ashley, **53**, 90
Vicksburg, Miss., 30
victims, 36, 80, 81
Virginia, 70, 95

W

Walker, John Hardeman, 4, 13
Ward, Bob, **49**
War Department, 37
wards, 85
Washington, George, 25
Waters, Richard Jones, 12, 68
Watson, Robert Goah, 4
Wayne County, Mo., 8
Webster County, Mo., 8
Weekly Record, 22, 30, 35, 36, **48**, **52**, **63**, 67, 77
Wentzell, David D., 72
West Swamp, 68
Whites Only sign, 70
Wilkins, Jess, **53**
Williams, Charles, 35

Winchester, Mo., 13, 14
Winchester, William, 13
Winsor, Elisha, 13
Winston, Laura Jackson, 27
Woman Suffrage Act, 28
women in combat roles, 89
Woodfin, Charles, 35
Woods, C.C., 24
Works Progress Administration (WPA), 29, 73
World War I, 3, 26, 77
World War II, 78
Wright County, Mo., 8
Wright, Erie, **53**

Y

Yount, F.R., ii

Z

Zimmerman, Orville, 37

www.ingramcontent.com/pod-product-compliance
Lightning Source LLC
Chambersburg PA
CBHW071225090426
42736CB00014B/2971